Losing Hurts
Twice as Bad

# Losing Hurts
# Twice as Bad

✧ ✧ ✧

## THE FOUR STAGES TO
## MOVING BEYOND IRAQ

Christopher J. Fettweis

W. W. NORTON & COMPANY

New York   London

For information about permission to reproduce selections from this book,
write to Permissions, W. W. Norton & Company, Inc.,
500 Fifth Avenue, New York, NY 10110

For information about special discounts for bulk purchases, please contact
W. W. Norton Special Sales at specialsales@wwnorton.com or 800-233-4830

Manufacturing by RRD Bloomsburg
Book design by Helene Berinsky
Production manager: Julia Druskin

Library of Congress Cataloging-in-Publication Data

Fettweis, Christopher J.
Losing hurts twice as bad : the four stages to moving beyond Iraq /
Christopher J. Fettweis. — 1st ed.
p. cm.
Includes bibliographical references and index.
ISBN 978-0-393-06761-3 (hardcover)
1. Iraq War, 2003– 2. United States—Politics and government—2001–
I. Title.
DS79.76.F475 2008
956.7044'30973—dc22
2008019795

W. W. Norton & Company, Inc.
500 Fifth Avenue, New York, N.Y. 10110
www.wwnorton.com

W. W. Norton & Company Ltd.
Castle House, 75/76 Wells Street, London W1T 3QT

1 2 3 4 5 6 7 8 9 0

for Lucy Kathleen

# CONTENTS

# ACKNOWLEDGMENTS

Tʜɪs ʙᴏᴏᴋ ʜᴀs benefited in no small measure from many conversations with my colleagues and students at the Naval War College. As I have repeatedly told anyone who will listen, no better place for the investigation of strategic issues exists. And there are no better people to work for than Joan Johnson-Freese and Tom Fedyszyn.

Neither they, nor the college, nor the Department of Defense can shoulder the blame for this book, however. The thoughts contained herein are my own.

I would like to thank the many people who have shaped my thinking about international politics over the years, especially John Mueller, George Quester, and the late Admiral William Crowe. In addition, several people were subjected to portions of this manuscript, and offered helpful comments and critiques. My thanks go to Robin Rauzi, Richard Pine, Robert Weil, Lucas

Wittmann, Robert Fettweis, and J. Celeste Lay for not being too tough on me.

Earlier versions of some of the book's arguments have appeared in the *Los Angeles Times*, *Survival*, and *Political Science Quarterly*.

Chris Fettweis

*Newport, RI*

*May 2008*

Losing Hurts
Twice as Bad

---

# Introduction

## SPARKY'S WISDOM

I N THE 1970s, Cincinnati was home to one of the greatest
teams in baseball history. The "Big Red Machine," as its Reds
were known, won two World Series titles with a combination of
future Hall-of-Famers, outstanding role players, and notorious
gamblers. One would think that the pleasure manager Sparky
Anderson took in his many victories would have outweighed the
pain of his few defeats. Most of us who watched them play probably don't remember them ever losing; still, they lost enough for
Sparky to observe that overall, "losing hurts twice as bad as winning feels good."

Sparky was describing a phenomenon that seems to be central to the human experience, one that applies with equal power
to baseball, finance, and love: As a general rule, human beings
are haunted by their failures to a far greater degree than they are
inspired by their successes. People, even enormously successful
people, tend to focus on the negative. War is no different. The

winners of World War I, for example, were far less affected by their victory than were the losers by their defeat. Celebrations ended in the North after the Civil War within a few months; the South, on the other hand, still has not forgotten. For reasons that are not entirely clear, while winning may make us happy for a brief moment, losing can bother us for a lifetime.

The psychological, social, economic, and political ramifications of military failure often dwarf what a rational calculation of cost would predict. The United States absorbed the loss in Vietnam quite easily on paper, but its effects linger to this day. The Afghanistan debacle was an underrated contributor to the Soviet malaise in the 1980s and a major factor in Mikhail Gorbachev's decision to embark upon *perestroika*, *glasnost*, and the other reforms that led to the collapse of the USSR. Defeat, even in seemingly little wars in inconsequential, far-away places, can often be quite traumatic.

Losing what by all rights should have been won is especially difficult to bear. As any athlete or sports fan can tell you, defeat is that much more painful when your team (or your country) is a heavy favorite going in. For every inspirational David, every tiny Milan High School that wins the Hoosier State Basketball Championship, there is a heartbroken Goliath, or a South Bend Central High. When victory is expected but does not materialize, supporters will demand explanations, and someone will have to shoulder the blame. Although military professionals and students of history know that when guerrilla forces have the support of the population they can be a particularly formidable foe, to the general public they do not appear to be much of a match for the regular armies of mighty nations. When guerrillas win—or, to be accurate, when they avoid losing for long enough that the bigger country concedes—the appearance of an upset is unavoidable.

How unfortunate it is that we insist on describing the outcome of wars using the same terms we use for sports. War is most certainly not a baseball game or a chess match, where one side emerges as the victor and the other the vanquished. To borrow a famous phrase, war is "politics by other means," not a competition of national will or evaluation of our worth. It is far better described with words like "success" or "failure" of policy goals, rather than "victory" or "defeat" of the nation. This is especially true of guerrilla wars, which rarely have neat, decisive outcomes and a clear "winner." The most likely outcome of the war in Iraq is prolonged, muddled ambiguity, rather than clear victory or defeat.

In the end, however, philosophical discussions about the nature of warfare will matter little. Whether appropriate or not, people interpret wars using competitive frameworks. Psychologists tell us that people are generally intolerant of ambiguity and complex judgments, preferring simple, familiar, binary categories.[1] In war, one side wins; the other loses. One side is showered in glory; the other, ignominy. The American public will therefore tend to view Iraq as a *lost war* rather than a *failed policy*, and the consequences for the national psyche are likely to be profound.

Technically speaking, of course, the United States cannot be defeated in Iraq. The U.S. military will never lose even the tiniest of battles against the various ragtag militias, terrorists, and resistance groups that have emerged in Saddam Hussein's wake. There will be no climactic, decisive engagements, and no dramatic surrenders in railroad cars or on board battleships. The war over the occupation will continue until the United States decides that it is no longer worth fighting. Just as Washington began this war at a time of its own choosing, it will also be the one to determine when it ends.

This does not mean that the war will end well, or soon. No matter when the United States decides to end this war, when the guns and bombs finally fall silent, peace will not bring "victory" in any meaningful sense. The war has been a political, economic, moral, humanitarian, and above all *strategic* disaster of the first order. The impossibility of an Appomattox, however, guarantees that the battle over its meaning and messages will rage for some time to come. For those guardians of patriotic correctness, the fact that there were no battlefield defeats will prove that the war was never really lost. But for a far greater proportion of the American people, the war in Iraq will be judged (correctly, in my view) to have been the worst kind of defeat for the United States: an *unnecessary* one, in a war that should never have been fought.

This is a book about the likely consequences of disaster in Iraq. It will separate the probable outcomes from the improbable for domestic politics, economics, and international security. It will not provide much discussion of why the war was fought, or how it was lost; already too many such sources exist. Instead of dwelling on the past, it will look to the future, using history only as a guide to judge what is likely to unfold. The United States is after all not the first country to lose after being a heavy favorite.

And despite the tone of the preceding paragraphs, the story is not entirely gloomy. While no functioning crystal balls exist, it seems likely that many of the most dire post-Iraq predictions are also among the least likely to occur. It is important, therefore, to recognize what history suggests will happen in the years ahead, and prepare ourselves to be able to adjust, recover, and begin to move on.

# Defeat in Iraq?

Is it not merely defeatism to be having such a discussion before the war is over? After all, in the closing months of 2007, many analysts began to make the case that Iraq was turning a corner, as a result of three major events that had taken place that summer. In declining order of significance, they were: The Sunni tribes in the provinces surrounding Baghdad turned against the al Qaeda–led, fundamentalist elements in their midst; Moktada al Sadr, the Shi'ite firebrand, called a cease-fire following a major incidence of Shi'ite-on-Shi'ite violence, and commanded his Mahdi Army to suspend its war against the occupier; and the United States "surged" thirty thousand troops into Iraq and changed its counterterrorism strategy. By some measures, and in some areas, the military situation improved rather dramatically. Anbar Province, which had been an al Qaeda/Sunni insurgent stronghold since the invasion, experienced an especially significant improvement in its day-to-day security. Casualty levels fell nationwide by about 60 percent during the autumn of 2007, among both Iraqi civilians and U.S. soldiers. The success of the early stages of the surge led a number of commentators—especially those who were the strongest supporters of the decision to go to war in the first place—to proclaim a whole new level of optimism about the war's potential to end on a rather successful note.[2]

However, despite the legend that grew around the military success of the surge, there was little improvement in the factors that matter most in determining whether Iraq would soon be able to function as a stable country. Somewhere between a quarter and half the population remained unemployed.[3] Iraq's state-run businesses, which were stunningly inefficient before the war, had been in disarray since the invasion.[4] The capital still lacked consistent power. Oil production languished below Saddam-era levels, when UN sanctions restricted the trade. Sectarian violence and ethnic cleansing, while perhaps past their peak, still raged at a higher pace than virtually anywhere else in the world. Iraq's army and police forces remained untrustworthy at best and overtly sectarian at worst. Corruption and crime occurred openly and without penalty. Finally, and most importantly, the Iraqi government remained farcical, unable to come to basic agreements on anything of real importance, despite years of effort, arguing, and extended vacations.

It is little wonder that as many as 2 million Iraqis fled their country, and an equal number remained internally displaced.[5] The enormous scale of the refugee crisis made it the worst in the history of the modern Middle East, surpassing the massive forced migrations of Palestinians and Israelis in 1948. Those who fled were of course those with the means to do so—the middle class, the doctors and lawyers and bureaucrats, the very people Iraqi society could have least afforded to lose. As time goes on, as they sink roots in their new homes, the likelihood of their return diminishes.

Iraq under Saddam Hussein's tyrannical mismanagement was a society teetering on the edge of the abyss; with its invasion, the

United States pushed it in. No matter how encouraging the security situation may be (and of course there may be some reason to doubt official U.S. optimism, as anyone who lived through the Vietnam era can attest), Iraq remains an economic, social, and political basket case. No amount of U.S. blood and treasure will be able to put this Humpty Dumpty back together again. From a humanitarian perspective, the invasion achieved the impossible: It made daily life for Iraqis, which was already awful under Saddam, even worse. The lone exception is in the north, where the Kurds have flourished, and are far better off than they were in 2002. Relatively insulated from the civil strife that engulfed the rest of the country, quasi-independent Kurdistan can now concentrate on national consolidation, economic development, and the exportation of terrorism to neighboring Turkey, a NATO ally of the United States.

The clearest signs of progress were in the fight against the al Qaeda–related groups. Since President George W. Bush consistently described Islamic fundamentalists as the main enemy in Iraq, it was little wonder that optimism abounded in some corners. However, al Qaeda in Iraq, which did not exist prior to the invasion, was never the main enemy of stability. In November 2006, Michael Hayden, director of the CIA, had listed al Qaeda as the *fifth* most pressing threat in Iraq.[6] The tenuous cease-fire that has occurred between the other warring groups hardly represented true reconciliation. Civil wars after all often include pauses that allow both sides to regroup and rearm.

If the United States is willing to occupy Iraq for long enough, many of its negative trends would probably be reversed. Given enough time, most societies usually recover from disaster. But even if our political leaders do manage to overrule public opinion and keep significant numbers of troops in place until Iraq recovers, the war will never be considered a success. No matter how the war finally comes to an end, it will not be possible to hide the utter pointlessness of this tragedy: By 2003, the profoundly weakened Saddam Hussein simply posed no threat whatsoever to American interests; he was not able to credibly threaten his neighbors, and even proved basically incapable of preventing the Kurds in northern Iraq from declaring de facto independence; he had no ties to Islamic fundamentalist terrorist groups, and there was no functioning al Qaeda presence in Iraq; and, most obviously, he possessed none of the dreaded weapons of mass destruction.

Just what was gained by the invasion? Iraqi democracy is an illusion, purple-fingered voters notwithstanding. Far from being undermined, Islamic fundamentalism is stronger than ever, thanks in large part to the ready-for-recruiting-poster images coming out of the carnage. The war did not begin a march toward liberalism and democracy in the Middle East that would have undercut support for al Qaeda, as neoconservatives promised. For the most part, democracy seems to have been weakened across the region as a result of the war.[7] Regional authoritarian governments have not only failed to liberalize but have cracked down on the democratic movements that were already discouraged by the debacle in Iraq. Iran is stronger, more influential, and far more conservative than it was prior to the invasion. America is nearly a trillion dollars deeper in debt, and the toll is mounting. Four thousand battle deaths and ten times that number of wounded have resulted in nothing of strategic importance to the United States. Every single significant outcome of this war has been negative. And it appears to be far from over.

Most important, no matter how successful the surge may prove to be, it is not likely to change public opinion. Consistent majorities of Americans think defeat is a forgone conclusion. *USA Today*/Gallup polls found that 60 percent of the country supported a rapid pullout of U.S. troops before General David Petraeus made the administration's case for more time; after his testimony, the number only dropped to 59.[8] Those who supported the war before the surge are the ones most convinced that the tide has turned in Iraq (which is a bit odd, since they generally were not convinced that the tide needed to be turned in the first place). Neoconservatives and right-wing talk show hosts went from being guardedly optimistic at the beginning of 2007 to ready for tickertape victory parades a year later. The majority of Americans, however, did not appear to believe that anything of importance had changed.

No democracy can long sustain a war without the support of its people, and a large and consistent majority of Americans have turned against continuing the fight in Iraq. Politicians, as usual, have followed, not led. Polls tell us that 2005 was the decisive year for this war, the year that the public decided that the struggle was no longer worth the cost. When respected senior Republican senators like Richard Lugar of Indiana and John Warner of Virginia decided that changes had to be made, the rest of the Congress could not have been far behind. Perhaps most important, there is no example of a modern democracy having changed its mind once it turned against a war. Once popular support for a war is lost, it is gone for good.⁹ After the Tet Offensive, for example, the American people were never again persuaded to lend their support for the war in Vietnam, no matter how events on the ground unfolded. There should be little doubt, therefore, that the end in Iraq is indeed in sight. Eternal occupation is neither politically, economically, nor morally sustainable.

Popular anger over the war has been driven in large part by the common perception that the war was fought under false pretenses. As politicians and commentators on the left continually asserted that "lies got us into Iraq," the general public began to ask two questions through gritted teeth: How did we get into that stupid war in the first place, and why was it such a disaster? The (correct) perception that the war was unnecessary is one of the main reasons why the public is unlikely to ever change its mind about the wisdom of continuing the struggle.

While it is not at all clear that actual prevarication was involved, there can be no doubt that the Bush administration shaped America's perceptions of this war almost as badly as it handled the tactics. The war was sold to a skeptical public from the beginning as a necessary step to keep America safe in a post-9/11 world. Saddam Hussein was stockpiling a variety of frightening weapons, some of which were eventually bound to kill our children. War was the right choice, we were told repeatedly, since we could not let the "smoking gun be a mushroom cloud." In other words, the war was sold with reference to a secondary purpose. The real reason for the attack—to create momentum for democracy in the Middle East and undercut the support for terrorism—was apparently deemed insufficiently terrifying.

When no superweapons were discovered—not even the poor man's WMD, the chemical and biological variety—the administration changed its terms. Bush administration officials could not help but appear to be remarkably disingenuous when they began to emphasize other goals, especially the spread of democracy and freedom, which may have been closer to the real strategic justification for the invasion but were rarely mentioned before it began. The administration thought it wiser to scare the American people into supporting the war rather than defend its grand strategic vision. It is unlikely, therefore, that the majority of the American people, not just those on the left, will ever be convinced that this war was anything but a disaster.

The best the United States can hope for—and even this appears to be a long shot—is to leave behind a functioning, stable Iraq, where a central government manages to hold together and stave off civil war, Islamic fundamentalism, and Iranian influence. In this best-case scenario, Iraq will not be a breeding ground for terrorists and will harbor no WMD programs. It will be able to provide power to its capital and other basic requirements for an acceptable minimum standard of living for its people, one which it cannot currently provide. In other words, *the best we can hope for is an Iraq that looks a great deal like the one we found in 2003*, only this time led by a strongman who may be a bit friendlier to the West. Rarely are wars that aim for what amounts to a return to the *status quo ante* considered worthwhile ventures. Post-surge optimism should therefore be kept in perspective. At best, this war may someday be judged as a rather inconsequential waste of American blood and treasure. At worst, it could be remembered as the greatest blunder in the history of the United States. The choices made over the course of the next few years will make the difference.

## The Meaning of Defeat

Since the endgame in Iraq is now clear, in outline if not detail, we ought to prepare ourselves for what will likely be an acrimonious stretch of time as U.S. society struggles to come to grips with the meaning of this disaster. The perception of defeat will loom over this war, and will probably throw American politics into a downward spiral of bitter recriminations the likes of which it has not seen in a generation. This country has not recovered from the Vietnam Syndrome, which continues to haunt American society and politics. The Iraq Syndrome is coming, whether we like it or not, and it is likely to do much the same.

The United States has lost only one war in its history. Nitpickers might insist that the War of 1812 wasn't exactly a glorious triumph, since after all the British did sack Washington, D.C., but one can at least make a plausible case that it (along with the war in Korea) ended in a face-saving tie. Only Vietnam ended badly for the United States. Lyndon Johnson used to worry about being the first president to lose a war; George Bush can only avoid being second by handing his war off to a successor. This appears to be the only exit strategy to which he has ever given serious contemplation.

In fact, administration officials have consistently argued that if they were given the opportunity to replay their actions, their decision to invade would remain unchanged. Vice President Dick Cheney haughtily dismissed suggestions that mistakes were made as "hogwash" and "dead wrong" since the "world is better off" without Saddam Hussein.[10] Perhaps they have little choice but to engage in such delusions as long as American men and women are risking their lives in the field. Perhaps, however, basic humanity (not to mention strategic wisdom) would demand just a bit of humility. After all, there is much blood on their hands.

It should surprise no one that the battle over the meaning of this disaster has begun in earnest. Both individuals and societies always feel the need to learn lessons from failure, in order to gain some sense of value from the troubled experience, and to assure themselves that their mistakes will not be repeated. The lessons America learns during this period will shape the future choices that the country will make, just as the lessons of Vietnam drove policy in its wake. Unfortunately, it is likely to prove difficult to hold a coherent strategic discussion in the immediate aftermath of Iraq. As the old saying goes, while victory has a thousand fathers, defeat is an orphan. The defining feature of the post-Iraq era will be intense partisanship, anger, and, to use a particularly awful post-Katrina neologism, "blamegaming." Soldiers are likely to come home to a starkly divided society.

Only by preparing itself for the natural divisiveness that follows defeat can the United States engage in an overdue self-examination in the aftermath of Iraq. We have to recognize the inevitability of intense emotion, and to the extent possible put it aside, in order to learn from this debacle. The people of the United States must be prepared to ask themselves a series of important questions, the answers to which will form the foundation of the lessons we draw from the war. When and where should the United States be willing to use force? What are our true national interests? Just how dire are the threats we face? How much influence can—or should—the United States really have in the far corners of the world? In other words, what is the proper grand strategy for the United States in the twenty-first century?

As we try to answer these questions over the course of this book, a few other themes will continually arise. One of the most important ones is the idea that *politics is, and always will be, the enemy of strategy.* Parties invariably place politics above national security, and people tend to judge foreign policy not on its merit, but by their attitude toward the party that espouses it. Republicans have always been more supportive than Democrats for all of President Bush's initiatives, for example. Similarly, Democrats were always more supportive of President Bill Clinton's policies, which in turn were opposed by the majority of Republicans. There is an especially strong correlation between support for the Iraq war and party identification, which is a dynamic that does not make for good strategy. In a very real sense, there is neither a Republican nor a Democratic foreign policy—there is only a U.S. foreign policy, and proper construction and evaluation cannot take place in an atmosphere dominated by partisanship and parochial concerns. In an ideal world, as the old saying goes, politics stops at the water's edge; in reality, it continues right across the oceans. Any suggestions for the way forward in Iraq will therefore be automatically opposed by about half of the American people. Party identification will prove more decisive than national interest. It will be quite difficult to hold a useful discussion of Iraq in such a highly politicized atmosphere.

Obviously, it would be naive to suggest that it is possible to keep politics completely separate from strategy, nor would it be fully desirable to do so in a democracy. But for the sake of this book, we will attempt to clarify the national interest by keeping the two realms separate, to the extent possible. The words "Republican" and "Democrat" will rarely appear in these pages; instead, we will examine ideas, arguments, and strategic alternatives.

The next theme of this book echoes Sparky Anderson: Losing hurts more than winning feels good. This phenomenon, which we will explore in some depth in the first chapter, has a few direct consequences. First, and most obviously, *the fear of losing often drives our policies in directions that are not necessarily in the national interest.* We will be tempted to persist in Iraq long beyond the point of usefulness, for the sake of victory itself. This fear of losing will skew our ability to judge the costs and benefits of continuing the effort to bring stability to the Persian Gulf. Another consequence of our aversion for losing is that *we consistently imagine that the consequences of losing will be far worse than what reality delivers.* As a nation we overreact to threats, preferring to believe the worst imaginable scenarios are also the most likely. From global warming to Y2K to bird flu to terrorism, Americans are quick to believe in the most catastrophic potential consequences that the human imagination can devise.

This is especially true for international politics. Since, as we all know, Americans have neither a historical memory nor any real clue about how the rest of the world operates, we have no way to separate the plausible outcomes from the cockamamie. Americans are liable to believe the most dreary, dire predictions about the future, no matter how improbable they may be. Iraq is unlikely to prove to be an exception to this rule. Domestically, Iraq will prove to be the most divisive issue this country has faced since

Vietnam; internationally, however, there is little reason to believe the various predictions of catastrophe. The disaster will certainly be next to irrelevant for U.S. national security and for global stability. And it probably won't be catastrophic for the people of the region, either.

Unfortunately, no one has displayed the typical American ignorance of history more plainly than those in the Bush administration. The execution of the war, in fact, was not nearly as bad as is commonly believed. All of the decisions made about how to fight were perfectly consistent with the strategic assumptions of its architects. There were plenty of troops to get the job done, as long as the Americans were greeted as liberators by Iraqis yearning to breathe free. The dismissal of the Iraqi army would have been irrelevant if the Iraqis were indeed able and eager to install immediately a functioning democracy. While the majority of foreign policy professionals did not share the strategic assumptions of the neoconservatives and feared that this war would turn out much the way it did, they did not have the ear of the inexperienced president. His strategists let him down.

The third theme of this book, therefore, is a bit of strategic guidance. We will examine the wisdom of some of the most fundamental assumptions supporting the current U.S. grand strategy. At the risk of spoiling a dramatic ending, it will hopefully be clear by the book's end that *the United States can afford to be far less active in foreign affairs than it currently is.* As it turns out, geopolitical inertia rather than national interest drives much of what we do. If the United States is to avoid Iraq-like debacles in the future, serious adjustments need to be made in the way we interpret threats, opportunities, and goals. The first step toward recovery from the Iraq Syndrome will be to learn from the war's many mistakes, and assure ourselves that they will never be repeated.

We were led into the Iraq morass not by evil people lying on behalf of oil companies but by poor strategists with a shallow, naive understanding of international politics. A grand strategy based on strategic restraint would far better serve the interests of both the United States and the world at large. Our founding fathers would be horrified at what this country has become. A return to our traditional strategic roots is long overdue. Only by changing its current path can the United States put the Iraq disaster behind it once and for all.

Restraint would be a very *realistic* grand strategy, at least as strategists understand the term. Realism, or *Realpolitik*, as the Germans say, is the most widely accepted explanation for how the world works among international relations professionals.[11] Realists are a rather unsentimental lot who seek to describe the world as it is, rather than how we would all like it to be. They generally believe that the countries of the world are locked in a perpetual competition for power and security, and that all countries, no matter what kind of government they have (democracy, dictatorship, or something in between), tend to identify their interests in the same way and act in similar manners. The task for leaders, therefore, is to identify and prioritize national interests, and devise methods to pursue them. Realists generally counsel against using force as part of Wilsonian moral crusades to spread democracy and freedom, except for those rare times that doing so would directly affect the interests of the United States. They are skeptical of claims that some states are inherently good and others evil; instead, they consider that the most significant difference between countries is in the amount of power—especially military power—that they possess.

Realists generally consider nationalism to be the most important motivating force in international politics. Over and over again throughout history, U.S. leaders have underestimated the power of nationalism, especially when compared to the attraction of freedom. The Johnson administration could not understand why so many people in Vietnam wanted the United States to leave, even though we were trying to bring them freedom and democracy. Likewise, President Bush was surprised at the ingratitude of the people of Iraq. As it turns out, people do not like to be conquered, even by foreigners who come with promises of democracy and freedom. Realists, however, were unsurprised. It is perhaps important to note that virtually all major international relations scholars and analysts opposed the invasion of Iraq from the beginning, and think that it has been an unmitigated disaster for the United States.[12] Realists in particular were skeptical of President Bush's plans to bring freedom to the Middle East, because they understood something that he and his neoconservative advisers apparently did not: even in the twenty-first century, nationalism still matters.

The book's final theme is also its most optimistic. Perhaps the most important consequence of our historical ignorance is the loss of overall perspective about the current era. Here at the beginning of the twenty-first century, the world is at a more peaceful and prosperous stage than ever before. Never have levels of warfare been lower, or development higher. Life expectancy and living standards are much greater than they were for all past generations. Major war is unthinkable, and minor ones are rare, despite the fact that the number of countries (and people) is far higher than ever before. The security threats facing humanity today—terrorism, drug gangs, rogue states, and so on—pale in comparison to the challenges faced by our predecessors. People from any previous time in human history would have been more than happy to trade their problems for ours. *We are living in a golden age*; but few people seem to notice. Instead, for many, catastrophic terrorist attacks and prolonged guerrilla quagmires represent chilling visions of things to come. Official signals, such as omnipresent color-coded threat warnings and mysterious recommendations to stockpile duct tape and plastic sheeting, add to the overall levels of anxiety. Six in ten Americans apparently believe that a third world war is "likely to occur" in their lifetime; others, including influential politicians, believe it has already begun.[13] Overwhelming majorities of people from all walks of life harbor the impression that the world is a far more chaotic, frightening, and ultimately more dangerous place than it was during the "simpler" times that came before.[14]

This impression, however widespread, does not match the facts. All of the evidence we have suggests that not only is the current era markedly better in most international security categories than at any time in history, but it is growing more peaceful and stable as time goes by. At the very least, to a growing number of experts, a major clash of arms does not seem plausible. But gradual, positive changes just do not seem to have the same cachet as catastrophic attacks and predictions of doom. Grim headlines, not optimistic trends, garner votes and sell newspapers, though they do not necessarily reflect reality. We ought to be significantly happier than we are, Iraq and 9/11 notwithstanding.

THE UNITED STATES is hardly the first great power in history to find itself facing military failure in a far-off, relatively minor war. In fact, it seems as if every powerful country has taken a turn being defeated by a manifestly inferior opponent. In the seventeenth century, Hapsburg Spain was the most powerful county in Europe, but it was unable to quash a revolt in the Netherlands. Over the course of eighty years of near-constant fighting, which included a good deal of guerrilla-style tactics throughout the boggy Low Countries, the Dutch were able to win their independence. The mighty Spanish Empire was never the same. A century later, the British faced a similar revolt that they were unable to put down in their New World colonies. France could not subdue the rebellious Algerians, who gained their independence in the mid-1960s. The United States took its turn in Vietnam; the Soviet Union, in Afghanistan. These experiences and more will constitute the precedents from which we can infer our lessons as we speculate about what is likely to happen after Iraq.

It is often said that history is written by the victors; in this book, we will let the vanquished tell their story. Many societies have suffered through periods of time far worse than what the United States will soon experience; surely there are lessons to be learned. In fact, there are a series of identifiable, predictable stages that societies typically go through following a defeat, which are in some ways similar to the familiar stages of grief that psychologists discuss following loss. First, the people of a nation experience shock and denial; next, they feel anger, toward their leaders, institutions, and the traitorous elements in their midst; third, they pass through a collective national depression. Finally, the nation will reach a level of acceptance if, and only if, it can come to grips with the reality of defeat. No national healing can begin without the recognition that the war has indeed been lost.

The disaster in Iraq is likely to affect American society and politics to a degree that is inexplicable by any rational examination of the facts. The domestic impact of Iraq is going to be profound; internationally, however, the story will be much different. Despite the conventional wisdom that defeat in Iraq would have long-lasting, serious consequences, there are good reasons to believe that the national security ramifications will be minimal. The United States will remain the world's most powerful and influential country, and it will continue to lead the world in the struggles against terror, tyranny, and poverty. During these dark domestic times to come, it will be important to focus on the material reality of post-Iraq America, which is not likely to be terribly different from that which came before. The United States will survive any outcome, even defeat, quite well. The American people need not fear losing, nor resist the withdrawal of their troops, since contrary to what they are constantly told, they will be just as safe, secure, and prosperous as they were before the misguided war began.

Sparky Anderson would certainly understand why losing in Iraq is going to hurt twice as bad as winning would have felt good. The United States is about to embark on its second great era of rancor, divisiveness, and vitriol caused by the perception of having lost a war to a manifestly inferior opponent. Like every nation (and team) that has come before, America is going to find it very difficult to deal with being upset. The Iraq Syndrome is coming, and we need to be prepared for the soul-searching, anger, self-doubt, and recrimination that will be its hallmarks. It will be the defining legacy of the Bush administration, and neoconservatism's parting gift to America.

# I

---◇---

# On Losing

Tate George knows that the agony of defeat weighs on our minds far more clearly than the thrill of victory. In 1990, George was the point guard for the University of Connecticut basketball team, which was making its first appearance in the season-ending championship tournament. In a third round game against Clemson, he hit a last-second, twenty-foot shot at the buzzer that propelled the Huskies into the final eight, putting UConn on the road to national greatness, where it has been ever since. George's shot was the most important single basket in the history of Connecticut basketball, and one of the most consequential in recent college basketball. Seventeen years later, however, George remembered little about it. "To tell you the truth," he told an interviewer, "I hardly think about it. What I think about more is what happened afterward."[1] In the next game against a powerhouse Duke team, a pass caromed off George's leg with just seconds to go and went out of bounds. Moments later,

Duke superstar Christian Laettner hit a shot to win the game, ending what had been easily UConn's most successful season to that point.

Even though his heroics put his team firmly on the path toward becoming a college basketball powerhouse, George remembers the loss in the next round far more clearly. His experience is quite typical, for athletes and non-athletes alike. "Most athletes have memories of losing the key game rather than winning it," explained the former Notre Dame football player Mike Oriard, who played on a number of winning teams himself during his career.[2] For Tate George, as for most of us, while glory is fleeting and hard to remember, ignominy is often impossible to forget.

Why should this be so? Wouldn't life be better if the opposite were true, if we quickly forgot the losses and the negatives and focused instead on our triumphs? Human beings, as it turns out, are not the most rational of creatures. We often seem to be motivated more by the fear of failure than the desire for victory—in games, love, finance, and war—and we react to defeat in seemingly inexplicable ways. Iraq will not likely prove an exception. Since a substantial portion of the American public will never consider the war to be a success, perhaps it would be worthwhile to spend a few moments reflecting on how people deal with losing in general, and military defeat in particular. Doing so should help Americans understand what is likely to lie ahead after Iraq.

## Prospect Theory and the Psychology of Losing

The psychologists Daniel Kahneman of Princeton University and Amos Tversky of Stanford University were among the first to investigate the implications of how we win and lose, and earned a Nobel Prize for their efforts. They developed what has become known as *prospect theory*, which helped explain how and why people react so disproportionately to losing.[3] Prospect theory is the academic expression of the phenomenon that concerned Sparky Anderson at the opening of this book: Losing hurts far more than winning feels good. A range of laboratory experiments has demonstrated that there is much wisdom in Sparky's observation. Over and over again, subjects have reported depths in satisfaction that are lower following losses than the height of peaks for equivalent gains. As a consequence, we are much more liable to choose more risky options when facing a potential loss, and less risky ones when facing a gain.

Theoretically, if we were rational, the pleasure we would take from winning would be roughly equivalent to the anguish we feel following loss. In practice, however, this is rarely the case. Losing ten dollars annoys us more than finding ten dollars makes us happy, for example. The devastation of lost love often far outweighs the joy that comes from a healthy relationship. Generally speaking, people are motivated more by the prospect of failure than by the potential for victory. To use the technical term, we are *loss-averse*.

Kahneman and Tversky found that people adjust quickly to a new status quo, and judge all consequent events according to that standard. For example, they discovered that people who won one hundred dollars and then lost fifty reported being less happy than those who merely won fifty, even though the net gain was the same. Human beings just do not appear to be hard-wired to remain too happy or too sad for long. The same process that allows us to recover after negative events (adaptation or "renor-malization") also limits the time that we experience pleasure when positive things occur.[4] Good fortune and improvements to our lives quickly become part of our status quo, the reference point through which we judge new information.[5] Losses, however, are far more difficult to accommodate. Rarely are people or nations content to accept less than they currently have, whether that is measured in money, lower living standards, or status. Grievances can last generations, as the sons of the Confederacy can attest. It is irrational, perhaps, but universal: Forward steps are soon for-gotten while those that go backward are remembered forever.

Prospect theory helps explain why we persist in losing ventures long after it is clear to any objective observer that the chances of success are slim. When defeat looms, fear overwhelms our abil-ity to make rational cost-benefit decisions, and we end up spend-ing good money after bad in the faint hope of reversing the tide. History is full of examples of countries that resisted sage advice to cut losses in wartime and move on. The Spanish crown persisted in its war against the Dutch in the 1600s long after its advis-ers had concluded that the war could not be won.[6] Four centu-ries later, the United States persisted in Vietnam for years after it became clear that the war was unwinnable, leading Defense Department official Fred Iklé to observe with resignation that it is "commonplace in human affairs that men continue to labor on major undertakings a long time after the ideas upon which these efforts were based have become obsolete."[7] Just because it is common, however, does not make it wise.

Loss aversion has a number of other effects. The innate fear of losing, for example, often makes people prone to believe that all sorts of catastrophes will follow defeat. The psychologist Ralph K. White called this the "non-rational inflation of anxiety," which makes the most negative of outcomes seem to be more likely than they really are.[8] Were we not disproportionately focused upon losses, we might be better at realistically assessing the threats we face. Instead, people tend to exaggerate the dangers in their lives, both as individuals and as societies. On the flip side, people often minimize (or completely fail to recognize) the importance of the positive changes that occur. The good times, and overall social progress, go underappreciated. "No matter how much better the present gets," observes the political scientist John Mueller, "the past gets better in reflection, and we are, accordingly, always notably worse off than we used to be. Golden ages, thus, do happen, but we are never actually *in* them: they are always back there somewhere (or, sometimes, in the ungraspable future)."[9] Rather than enjoy the advantages of their current situation, people instead tend to focus on how things could soon go terribly wrong.

Examples of our tendency to blow threats out of proportion are not hard to find. The "Y2K crisis" of the end of the last century was going to bring global computer systems to their knees, and perhaps launch Russian nuclear missiles. Consumers were threatened by cyanide in Tylenol and razor blades in Halloween candy; now, they have to beware of lead in Chinese-made toys and germs on ATMs. Americans are hardly the only ones to overreact to potential dangers. Europeans worry obsessively, and without apparent justification, about dangers lurking in genetically engineered food.[10] Overreaction to disease is perhaps a category all its own: Humanity has recently been threatened by the swine flu, then by SARS, then by West Nile, then by the bird flu.[11] As it turned out, none of these presumed superbugs proved to be very dangerous (at least not yet).

Those ringing alarm bells over global warming, which looms as the current environmental disaster *du jour*, ought to take pause and realize that if history is any guide, their worst fears are probably overblown as well. That the earth is warming due to human activity is doubted only by a Luddite fringe of right-wing talk radio hosts, pseudoscientists, and reactionary members of the House of Representatives; the science behind climate change is not really open to much rational debate at this point. What is less clear is the extent to which catastrophe will follow. The potential consequences of climate change are invariably expressed in the most hyperbolic ways: Rapidly rising seas, ice ages, catastrophic hurricanes, drowned polar bears, and all manner of disaster have been predicted to accompany the warming planet. The alarmism of even the current chief scientific adviser to the British government, who recently predicted that "Antarctica is likely to be the world's only habitable continent by the end of this century if global warming remains unchecked," evidently knows no bounds.[12] Pentagon planners and otherwise staid observers of foreign affairs see the potential for increased conflict, even nuclear war, due to climate change.[13] The planet is in peril, we are told, and we ought to be worried. Very worried in fact, according to a *Time* magazine cover story.[14]

It should go without saying that the planet's existence is not "in peril." The earth will survive in one form or another quite well, whether or not there are people able to live upon it. Moreover, there is little doubt that people will be able to continue to exist, and plenty of room for hope that we will be able to adjust over time to our warming climate. Humanity found ways to deal with prior environmental crises, from the disappearing ozone layer to acid rain. What Al Gore's influential film *An Inconvenient Truth* conveniently omitted was the wide disagreement in the scientific community about the likelihood of his predictions (although not, certainly, about the film's overall message). The film shows the *most extreme* potential consequences of climate change as if they were scientific consensus, presumably because they are the ones most likely to inspire action. But they are also not very likely. As the environmentalist Bjorn Lomborg explained in his important book *Cool It: The Skeptical Guide to Global Warming*, there is a growing consensus within the scientific community in the other direction, one that doubts many of the most commonly discussed consequences of climate change, from flooding to ice ages. Our biggest imagined disasters of climate change are not likely to occur, at least not to the drastic extent portrayed in the film. Gore claims that "at stake is the survival of our civilization and the habitability of the Earth."[15] In fact, both will probably come through the coming decades just fine. Climate change is certainly a serious problem, one that demands far greater official attention than it currently gets, but it is not likely to spell the end of humanity. It is partially our fear of losing—losing status, losing our lives, losing living standards—that makes us susceptible to believe that such unlikely catastrophes are imminent. It is simply too soon to buy property in Antarctica.

Terrorism is perhaps the most prominent, and most consequential, of our current overblown dangers.[16] Terrorists can certainly kill people and scare many more, but the damage they cause is more psychological than physical, and is in no way capable of changing the character of Western civilization. Only the people of the West, largely through their own overreaction, can accomplish that. Far from being an "existential" threat to our existence, terrorists are at best a nuisance (albeit an occasionally deadly nuisance) to the powerful countries of the world. Islamists in particular are often compared with the great enemies of the past, from the Nazis to the Communists, which elevates the potential danger they pose well beyond their capabilities. President Bush has repeatedly used the label "Islamo-fascists" to describe the enemy that our defense establishment has been reoriented to fight, as if the two terms had anything at all in common.[17] At any other time in history, Islamist terrorism would have been seen for what it is: a second-order threat, one that does not deserve to be elevated in status by the strongest country in the world; yet politics have dictated otherwise. We will return to this topic as the book unfolds.

It is commonplace to blame an overactive, omnipresent "media" for our propensity to exaggerate the potential for negative outcomes and disaster. Certainly the messages in the media do indeed exacerbate our worst-case-scenario thinking, since, as the saying goes, if it bleeds, it leads. But such media scaremongering would not be popular, or an easy way to sell papers and attract viewers, were we not predisposed to be fearful of the catastrophic consequences of losing. The media might profit from our paranoia, but it is hardly the cause. Our loss aversion predates CNN.

LOSING WARS

Few events are as traumatic to societies as military failure. Losing wars, even small wars in far-away lands, inevitably causes rather extreme social and psychological stress. The experience is not always wholly negative—indeed, some countries seem to wear defeat like a badge of honor, as a sign of shared suffering and mutual sacrifice in a noble, doomed cause. A 1389 disaster at the hands of the Turks is one of the seminal events in the Serbian cultural memory, as the United States discovered during the war in Kosovo. Shia Muslims still commemorate their loss to the Sunnis at Karbala in 680 as if it happened yesterday. And the experience of defeat in the Civil War is one of the key features that differentiates Southern identity from that of the rest of the United States.[18] Victory might bring accolades and glory, but defeat usually provides greater motivation for future generations.

Not all defeats are created equal, of course. There is a significant difference between losing what might be thought of as a total war, one that results in the destruction of the state, and a limited war in a distant land. Sometimes wars can be total for one side and peripheral to the other. The war in Vietnam obviously looked quite a bit different from Washington than it did from Saigon, where the stakes were far higher. Citizens of societies on the losing end of total wars historically have had more pressing issues to worry about than dealing with the frustration over defeat, such as where they are going to live, where their next meal will come from, and/or how long they are likely to survive as slaves.

As it turns out, national reactions to disastrous wars are fairly predictable. It is difficult to speak about how an entire nation will react to any particular event, and individual reactions to military failure vary especially widely. Some people merely report relief that the suffering has come to an end, especially after a long and costly struggle, and seem to be beyond caring much about who has won and who has lost. Others seem to be unable to put the event behind them, and carry the pain to their graves. Many people in the United States who lived through the Vietnam era still actively harbor anger over the outcome, for example, while others appear to be completely oblivious to the event, which seemed to have little effect on their lives. And of course those who have lost loved ones or been injured by conflict exhibit reactions far different from those who only suffer indirectly. To generalize individual reactions to an entire society is to risk making what political scientists refer to as a "level of analysis" mistake: What applies to the individual does not automatically apply to the collective. When doing this type of analysis, therefore, one must proceed with caution in order to avoid confusing the nation with its component parts. But proceed we will.

## Stages of National Grief

Tolstoy famously observed that while happy families are all alike, every unhappy family is unhappy in its own way. The same is true for countries following a war: Victory looks the same from culture to culture, but all countries seem to handle losing somewhat differently. Defeat is never exactly the same twice. Nonetheless, there are some elements that seem to appear with some regularity. In fact, the trauma that societies experience following a lost war can perhaps be grouped into stages that are somewhat similar to those that individuals pass through after a personal trauma or loss. Defeated nations experience their own version of the "stages of grief."

In her book *On Death and Dying*, Elisabeth Kübler-Ross identified five stages that a patient goes through after being informed of a terminal prognosis. First, he or she experiences denial (*this isn't happening to me*), which is followed by a period of anger (*this is not fair*). In the third stage, bargaining, the patient looks for a way out of the predicament by offering to make a deal, often with God, perhaps to be a better person if he or she survives. When the deal is not accepted, the patient proceeds to a period of depression, which is followed eventually by a measure of resignation and acceptance to what fate has in store.[19]

Over the years, these stages have been applied to a variety of different situations by researchers seeking insight into how people deal with loss or disappointment. I see a version unfold every time I hand back a test or paper. Students who receive grades that are worse than they expected tend to experience a modified, mild version of these stages. At first they are shocked, and unable to say much at all; then, they get angry (*the professor is a jerk, and he's always hated me*); before long, the anger gives way to bargaining, which for the professor is the most tiresome of the stages (*Can you take another look at my answer for number four? Can't you reconsider my essay answer, and give me one more point so I can get a B minus and keep my scholarship?*). Eventually, depression sets in. After a while, the student comes to accept the grade. Often all five stages unfold over the course of one class period, right in front of my eyes. By the time students leave the room, many have moved on to acceptance and are ready to put the test behind them. Others will need a few more days to complete the process. I warn them not to come to me to discuss the grade until they have moved into the final, more rational "acceptance" stage. No one benefits from a confrontation while the student is still in the throes of anger.

Countries seem to go through similar stages after military failure. Over the coming years, we can expect the United States to pass through four distinct stages as it deals with the disaster in Iraq. First, American society will experience a phase of shock and denial. Second, we will go through a period of national anger, which will be soon followed by extended depression. Finally, if history is any guide, we will move on to acceptance—and healing. Only through an understanding of these stages can their symptoms be recognized, and their corrosive effects minimized.

Generally speaking, the duration of these post-defeat stages is related to the decisiveness of defeat. In one-sided disasters like those that befell France in 1870 (following the Prussian siege and capture of Paris in the Franco-Prussian War) and Russia in 1905 (following its defeat in the Russo-Japanese War), the four stages are obvious, stark, and immediate. For more drawn-out disasters, the symptoms unfold more slowly, almost imperceptibly, and can vary widely from person to person. It might take years for some Americans to get to the final stage in the aftermath of Iraq, where the war can be considered and analyzed somewhat dispassionately; others may never quite get there. But for the majority of Americans, final acceptance of the disaster is not far off. The effects of the Iraq Syndrome are likely to be temporary, if not exactly brief, and they will not be debilitating for the nation as a whole.

## Stage 1: Shock and Denial

In the opening scenes in *Gone With the Wind*, members of the Southern gentry express full confidence in their ability to win the war that the Northern states have been foolish enough to thrust upon them. Despite the Union's manifest superiority in every measurable category, the plantation owners gathered in Ashley's mansion harbor no doubts that moral factors will lead the South to victory. "One Southerner can lick twenty Yankees," one man says; another points out that "gentlemen can always fight better than rabble." Rhett Butler tries to provide a skeptical voice of reason ("All we've got is cotton, slaves—and arrogance"), but he is drowned out by a chorus of fervor from hawkish Southern patriots. This fictional scene was an accurate reflection of the attitude with which the South entered the Civil War, and the way that most countries have gone to war throughout history. After all, we are invincible, once we put our minds to it.

Victory is easy to understand. It is what is expected, and only logical, given our obvious superiority to the opponent. As the cultural historian Wolfgang Schivelbusch once observed, "nations are as incapable of imagining their own defeat as individuals are of conceiving their own death."[20] Indeed, at the outset of war, even when the odds are stacked against us, victory usually seems certain to all but the most treasonous. Few countries embark on military adventures less than fully confident of victory. The millions of men who marched to war in August 1914 may have come from many different countries, but they shared the conviction that they would all be home by Christmas, showered in the reflected glory of battlefield success. In World War I, as is the case with most wars, one overconfident prewar society was proven wrong by events. When defeat comes, it is invariably shocking, devastating, and difficult to acknowledge. In the immediate aftermath of defeat, people usually take pains to avoid letting its reality sink in. The first post-defeat stage, therefore, is denial.

In 1967, the United States was typically confident about its ability to defeat the Viet Cong. General William Westmoreland told his men that they were destined for victory, since "We're smarter . . . we have more endurance and more to fight for . . . and we've got more guts."[21] The war's outcome, of course, proved him wrong. In its immediate aftermath, during the denial phase, few in the United States showed much interest in discussing the war. The historian George Herring referred to this period as "a self-conscious, collective amnesia." The war was all but ignored by the media for some time, and was hardly mentioned at all during the presidential campaign of 1976.[22] To an uninformed newcomer to the United States in the mid-1970s, it would have appeared that no war had ever been fought in Southeast Asia.

In this initial stage, people often seek refuge in the frivolous as part of their effort to push the seriousness of military failure as far from their minds as possible. National distractions take forms that seem as far removed from warfare as possible, such as art, music, or dancing. Spontaneous dance manias broke out in France in 1789 among the upper classes, who lost a great deal during the Revolution, and across Germany in 1919. As one French diarist noted in 1870, as a wave of dancing swept over Paris following defeat in the Franco-Prussian War, "France is dancing . . . as a form of revenge. It is dancing to forget."[23] Anything that serves to help the shocked masses forget what just occurred serves as a welcome relief during the denial stage. Perhaps it is no coincidence that disco followed Vietnam (which, to many people, merely piled one disaster on top of another).

The extent of the shock is directly related to two factors: the speed of defeat and the initial expectation of victory. Those on the business end of swift, catastrophic, unexpected disasters can exhibit symptoms of deepest shock. When French armies were rapidly swept from the battlefield by Prussians in 1870, for example, the French people went into a national state of denial and shock, which soon gave way to mania, rioting, and the seizure of Paris by Communard radicals. Tens of thousands died when the French army retook the capital two months later.[24] When war drags on to the point where the outcome is clear to all involved, however, the shock can be relatively minimal. Few in the American South were too surprised by the outcome of war by 1865; and Germans in 1945 could not have been shocked when their nation surrendered. In both cases the inevitability of defeat had long been clearly visible to all but the most fanatically optimistic.

The second factor related to the depth of shock is the extent to which victory is expected to occur. Failure is more acceptable when the nation was facing steep odds. In fact, such defeats are often seen as heroic, and form the stuff of legend. No national shock or other stages of grief followed the fall of the Alamo, for instance, or the defeat of the famous three hundred Spartans at Thermopylae. Defeat in the face of overwhelming odds implies no loss of honor—in fact, the mere act of trying, of resisting, is often seen as honorable in itself. When the odds seem to be with our side, however, when the experts expect a rapid victory but none materializes, the shock can be especially acute.

The war in Iraq exhibited one of these two factors for the United States: There were very high expectations of victory at the beginning of the war, but its resolution has certainly not been swift. This war was, after all, supposed to be easy, a "cakewalk," according to its neoconservative cheerleaders.[25] The American people were assured that our troops would be greeted as liberators by throngs of adoring wannabe democrats.[26] President Bush did not worry about the inability to rally the rest of the world to the cause, telling Secretary of State Colin Powell that "at some point, we may be the only ones left. That's OK with me. We are America."[27] Prominent hawks Richard Perle and David Frum argued that we ought to harbor no doubts about either the righteousness or the ease of the mission. "We should toss dictators aside," they wrote, "with no more compunction than a police sharp-shooter feels when he downs a hostage-taker."[28] The administration foolishly set expectations so high that virtually any level of difficulty would almost inevitably have been seen as resulting from its own incompetence.

However, while the intensity of the denial is likely to be increased because the United States will be upset by a seemingly inferior foe, its power will be substantially mitigated by the extended duration of the disaster. The national denial might even decrease to the point that it proves almost imperceptible, since there is not likely to be a precise moment after which we can say with confidence that the war is actually over. Iraqi insurgents are unlikely to ever raise a "Mission Accomplished" banner over the decks of one of their aircraft carriers any time soon. Defeat in Iraq will be devoid of sound and fury; because of this, the United States will probably avoid some of the most common experiences typical to nations in the first stage of the post-disaster recovery process.

## Stage 2: Anger

After emerging from the initial shock and denial that follow disaster, nations typically move on to more pernicious, destructive phases. Losses must be explained, and someone held responsible. Anger grows within the body politic, anger that needs an outlet, an object upon which to focus. Two main reactions are common: Some people resist blaming their country, and focus their rage instead upon a variety of traitorous guilty parties. It rarely proves difficult to identify scapegoats upon whom to pin the defeat. Other people hold the nation itself responsible, and seek to create as much psychological distance between themselves and their country as possible. Levels of patriotism, and optimism about the future, drop precipitously during this stage as the pride that people had previously taken in their country erodes. What is true for spectator sports is also true for spectator wars: Few people enjoy being closely associated with a loser.

## SCAPEGOATING ("BLAMEGAMING")

Defeated nations often enter this phase of collective anger much more rapidly than their leaders would prefer, since popular ire usually initially focuses upon the regime in power. Politicians seem to know that this will be the case, which helps explain why they are often among the last ones to admit defeat. Unless that anger is quickly deflected, the regime can be in serious danger of collapse.[29] Upset defeats have led to the collapse of a number of seemingly strong leaders, from the British government under Lord North in 1783 after the loss of the colonies, to the French Fourth Republic in 1958 during the Algerian disaster, to the Soviet Communist Party following failure in Afghanistan. Rage at those responsible for Vietnam grew in the United States as the war dragged on, and peaked with the Watergate scandal. Governments are always held

responsible for the underperformance of their armies on the battlefield, and for defeats major and minor.

Defeat often exacerbates standing societal discontent, which is
rapidly directed at leaders. In 1905, when the underdog Japanese
crushed the Russian fleet and army, Czar Nicholas II became the
focus of an already unhappy population. A revolution broke out
across Russia, in major cities and in small towns, which carried the
sympathy of large parts of the military. Eventually the czar was
forced to make a series of concessions in order to save his government, the most humiliating of which was the establishment of a
new legislature, or Duma, that would share power. The Romanov
dynasty was never the same.

Nearly six decades earlier, in 1848, the fragile Mexican government was thrown into deep turmoil following defeat by the United
States. The Mexican-American War is not often taught in history
classes on this side of the Rio Grande, but Mexican children all
learn that 500,000 square miles, or 40 percent of their country,
including what is today California and the American Southwest,
was forcibly taken from them after U.S. troops marched into
Mexico City. This humiliating, swift disaster led to decades of
political and social instability in Mexico, which included dictatorships, revolutions, civil war, ethnic conflict, and eventually
conquest by the French. The defeat was a decisive moment in
Mexican history.

The political leadership shoulders the initial blame for defeat,
but the military usually cannot escape unscathed. Generals usually become the second target of popular ire, which is often readily encouraged by the politicians. The list of military scapegoats is
as long as history itself, running from Nicias and Crassus through

to Ludendorff and Westmoreland. "Can Washington be called the conqueror of America?" asked a Loyalist judge after fleeing to London after the Revolution. "By no means. America was conquered in the British parliament. Washington could *never* have conquered it. British Generals *never* did their duty."[30] With better military leaders, the thinking goes, the nation might have escaped humiliation.

Anger over defeat often lasts longer than the governments that led their nations to disaster and the military leadership that underperformed. Defeated societies soon find other targets at which to direct their rage, groups of traitors in their midst, scapegoats that have let the country down in a variety of ways and opened the doors to defeat. Jews have of course been history's most popular target for irrational rage, but they have not been alone. Societies have been stabbed in the back over the years by socialists, pacifists, cowards, incompetents, hippies, the media, the political opposition, Freemasons, and every other imaginable group that is present in, but separate from, the mainstream of society. Often there is plenty of blame to go around.

The enemy never defeats us—we defeat ourselves. According to those patriots on the right, our strength is always too great for any foe to overcome. If our proud nation has fallen, it must have been betrayed from within. The Allies did not defeat Germany in World War I, for instance. The German national will to fight was actually undermined by a traitorous domestic coalition of anti-war forces; socialists in the parliament emboldened the enemy with discussions of armistice; defeatists in uniform questioned the wisdom of their leaders; mothers in Hamburg inexcusably allowed starvation to cloud their patriotism; and, of course, the Jew profited from surrender. In 1918, Germany was stabbed in the back. The *Dolschstoss* (stab-in-the-back) legend was born.

The legend reemerges, in somewhat different forms, virtually every time any nation loses a war. In 1940, France was stabbed in the back by Marshal Pétain and the Vichy collaborators; Charles de Gaulle returned the favor two decades later by abandoning Algeria. The noble American war effort in Vietnam was undermined by a variety of traitors, including liberal Democrats, campus hippies, the media, and Jane Fonda. If only the Congress had not cut the annual aid to South Vietnam by a third, so the argument goes, South Vietnam would probably be a flourishing democracy today. Unfortunately, the United States was stabbed in the back.

Preliminary and secondary outlets for popular anger following the disaster in Iraq seem to have already been identified. Initially, as always, political leaders have shouldered the brunt of the blame. In the case of the Bush administration's folly, this anger was fully justified, given the level of mismanagement and incompetence that it has demonstrated in Iraq. It is unlikely that those on the left in particular will ever divert the focus of their anger away from their leaders.

Other people have identified second and third targets for their anger. As usual, the military has followed the politicians as scapegoats for disaster. People from all points along the political spectrum agreed about the abject incompetence of the civilian leadership in the Rumsfeld Pentagon. The uniformed military received much less initial criticism than is usually the case with disastrous wars, which is a bit puzzling, given how poorly prepared the military was for what unfolded. We did not have the army we wish we had, to paraphrase Donald Rumsfeld, and that is the fault of the force planners in the Pentagon. To say that General Tommy Franks will not go down in history as one of our great commanders is a gross understatement.

Overall, the war's military commanders, especially those who were in charge at the beginning, will likely not be able to escape scrutiny forever. The generals have not yet been the target of Bush administration officials, but that will change when Rumsfeld, Wolfowitz, Feith, and the rest publish their memoirs. No doubt we will be told that our military leaders have screwed up what was otherwise a well-planned, necessary, and potentially glorious war. It will not be entirely fair criticism, of course, since the important decisions were made over their heads, and their advice was generally unwelcome or ignored. Loyalty, not honesty, led to promotions in the Rumsfeld Pentagon, which helps explain why by 2003 the senior military leadership was so eager to tell the president what he wanted to hear. Those who offered advice that did not fit the administration's game plan, like General Eric Shinseki, who had the temerity to suggest that somewhere between three and four hundred thousand troops would be necessary to pacify Iraq, were quite publicly shuffled off to retirement.

One of the highest priorities of any defeated administration is to deflect anger away from itself as quickly as possible, and the Bush administration has proven to be no different. By the fall of 2007, it became clear that the administration had identified a host of other potential scapegoats. Over the course of that summer, the surge laid the foundation for a plausible-sounding claim that a *Dolschstoss* for the war in Iraq was perpetrated by three related, and perhaps mutually reinforcing, elements. First, and most obviously, the Democrats (aided by their liberal media co-conspirators) stabbed America in the back. Just as Nixon and Kissinger were consumed by the desire to have their enemies on the left seem responsible for the defeat in Vietnam, Bush was eager to force the Democratic Congress to pull the final plug on the war.[31] Blaming the political opposition is of course a process as old as defeat itself. Political partisanship will be dealt with in some depth later, since it is likely to become one of the defining features of the coming Iraq Syndrome.

Second, perhaps popular anger can be directed toward the incompetent, untrustworthy, shortsighted, corrupt, infantile Iraqi ingrates who were unable to grasp the unprecedented opportunities that the Bush administration's faith-based foreign policy granted them. The Maliki government proved to be particularly galling in its failures to separate parochial religious and tribal interests from the good of the nation. The Iraqis were never able to cobble together a functioning national government; without a strong center, centrifugal forces tore the country asunder. Democracy was offered by America, or so the story goes, but in the final analysis a state has to seize freedom or it is doomed.

Third and far more damaging was the administration's obsession with the "meddling" of Iraq's neighbors. While one might think that it should have been rather unsurprising that Syria and Iran took an interest in the course of events in Iraq, the Bush administration reacted as if such interest is not only unforgivable but a possible *casus belli* for the next war on evil in the Persian Gulf. The final act of this tragedy may have not yet been written.

The recent tactical success has given neoconservative morale a boost, and in the mind of the hawks, justified their faith in victory. Although the ultimate outcome of the war is still not in doubt, the surge has served a very useful purpose for those who supported this war: It provided them rhetorical ammunition with which to defend their otherwise indefensible strategic choices. Historians on the right will someday be able to argue that defeat was once again snatched from the jaws of victory. The war had finally turned a corner, we will be told. The proper tactics were finally being employed when traitors pulled the rug out from under the war effort. Those politicians who demanded a draw-down of forces undercut the United States at the very moment that victory was within its grasp. The disaster can now be blamed on those who asked questions, emboldened our enemies, and stabbed America in the back. The foundation for a new *Dolschstoss* legend has been laid.

"In so many crises of war termination," former DoD official Fred Iklé observed a generation ago, "hawks have grossly neglected threats to the political future of their nation in stubborn pursuit of some secondary objectives. . . . Starting out as the defenders of the national interest, they wind up by trading their kingdom for a distant province. And in the end, when the kingdom is lost, they blame their 'dovish' opponents for having stabbed them in the back."[32] There is little reason to believe that the debate in the aftermath of the Iraq war will prove any different. The surge may have aided the cause of Iraqi unity, but it will almost certainly leave a more divided, angry America in its wake. Any victories it produces will ultimately be Pyhrric.

## "BLASTING"
The nation's prestige is also our personal prestige; its honor is our honor. When our country is victorious, we file into the streets and

celebrate our glorious victory. When it loses, we share the agony of defeat, whether or not we had actually suffered in any serious way while it raged. No one wants to be associated with a loser, whether it be a team, a presidential candidate, or a nation. Just as fans of losing teams stop going to games, citizens of losing countries lose faith in those who brought shame upon them.

Psychologists tell us that fans of unsuccessful sports teams react in two ways, both of which are designed to protect their personal sense of well-being. Many simply decrease their association with the losing team. We all know these "fair weather" fans who jump off the bandwagon at the earliest sign of trouble, or who only attend games when the team is winning. After their team's stunning defeat at the hands of lowly Division 1-AA Appalachian State in 2007, for example, many fans of the Michigan Wolverines simply spent their Saturday afternoons doing other things.

Not everyone can turn off their passions so easily, however. For die-hard fans, abandoning their team is not an option. A group of sports psychologists recently noted that these "highly identified" fans typically "experience depression and an intense negative affective state and adopt a poor outlook on life subsequent to their team's defeat."[33] This would not be news to my wife, who has seen me after too many Notre Dame football losses to count. Before long I begin to get mad at everyone, from the coach to the referee to the fifth-year senior captain center who insisted on snapping the ball over the quarterback's head. I experience what is known as "blasting," or "derogating an individual or group to regain one's psychological health."[34] By acting in a hostile manner toward others, the spectator can assert his or her psychological dominance, and restore some sense of personal well-being.

Alas, citizens of a defeated country cannot merely switch allegiances to another when theirs underperforms. They can however turn inward, downplay their patriotism, and stop taking pride in their nation. Blasting is therefore a common reaction during the second post-defeat stage. Nowhere was this phenomenon more clear than in post–World War II Germany, where displays of patriotism were generally considered to be distasteful and remain rare to this day. The Germans, of course, have additional reasons to feel somewhat ambiguous about being German, but blasting occurs in every society that loses a war. Levels of patriotism and confidence in the direction in which United States was headed were very low in the 1970s after Vietnam, and dropped again following the invasion of Iraq. In April 2008, 81 percent of Americans told CBS/ *New York Times* pollsters that they believed "things have pretty seriously gotten off on the wrong track."[35] Patriotism ceases to have as much meaning for people in defeated societies, many of whom seek for meaning in their lives in other (perhaps more productive) areas.

## WOUNDED ANIMALS AND SHORT-TERM DANGERS

Defeated countries in the anger stage are like wounded animals. During this time, they are in danger of reacting violently in the face of otherwise minor dangers or insults. Many leaders eager to demonstrate increased resolve in the immediate aftermath of defeat have throughout history proven to be even more willing to use force than they were before.[36] It was no coincidence that Philip III ordered the expulsion of the Moors in Spain on the very day that a humiliating, temporary truce in the war against the Dutch was signed.[37] Henry Kissinger wrote in his memoirs that in the aftermath of the Cuban missile crisis, the Soviet Union "launched itself on a determined, systematic, and long-term program of expanding *all* categories of its military power."[38] The United States will have to beware of the temptation to allow its wounded pride and humiliation to encourage it to act rashly in the aftermath of Iraq.

This dynamic was certainly evident following the fall of Saigon. The seizure of the merchant ship *Mayaguez* by the Khmer Rouge, which occurred in May 1975, provided the opportunity to demonstrate that the United States should not be trifled with. The response of the Ford administration was rapid, decisive, and belligerent. The president said at the time that he had to "show some strength in order to help us . . . with our credibility in the world." Kissinger had told reporters off the record that "the United States must carry out some act somewhere in the world which shows its determination to continue to be a world power." He wanted to react rapidly, arguing that "indecision and weakness can lead to demoralized friends and emboldened adversaries." Even though a rapid military response might have put the captured men at risk, their lives were unfortunately a "secondary consideration," argued Kissinger, since the "real issue was international credibility and not the safe return of the crew."[39]

The operation was a fiasco. By the time the attack began, the thirty-nine hostages had already been released unharmed; when it was over, forty-one American servicemen lay dead. From a military standpoint it was a minor disaster, marred by poor intelligence and execution. Still, polls suggest that the operation was popular with an American public that was still smarting in the aftermath of Vietnam. The operation provided a salve for the nation's open wounds, and 79 percent of the American people considered it to be a success.[40] In 1978, national security adviser Zbigniew Brzezinski commented privately to Senate staff members that he wished the Carter administration could have a *Mayaguez* incident so the president could "get tough with the communists."[41]

Iran now finds itself in the crosshairs of a wounded United States. Its meddling in Iraq, nuclear weapons program, and support for terrorism have the far right itching to use military force both to reassert U.S. credibility and to bring a (perhaps only temporary) halt to Iranian weapons development. Norman Podhoretz, the neoconservative patriarch, has written "The Case for Bombing Iran";[42] the title of former UN Ambassador John Bolton's new book reminds us that *Surrender Is Not an Option*, evidently meant for those of us who might otherwise be under the impression that surrender was in fact a legitimate option. The war drums are beating.

For neoconservatives, Iran is to Islamo-fascism what the Soviet Union was to communism: the enemy's epicenter, the origin and supporter of most of the world's evil. Ronald Reagan was surely not the only one who thought the Soviets were the root of all the world's ills. Without Moscow's interference, the Gipper proclaimed, "there wouldn't be any hotspots in the world."[43] The same kind of language and logic is currently being applied to Tehran, which has ascended to the position of anchor state for the forces of darkness. Then as now, pundits from the far right explain that they bear no animus toward the people of the enemy state, merely their oppressive government. Once the people were empowered to rid themselves of their rulers, world evil would recede into the night. As another of neoconservatism's senior intellectuals, historian of the Ottoman Empire Bernard Lewis, put it, either "we bring them freedom, or they destroy us."[44]

*Realpolitik* would counsel a different course. A realist might even suggest that Iran actually has legitimate security concerns and is acting somewhat rationally, given its geographic vulnerability. And that realist might wonder just exactly how Iran, with its comparably pathetic economic and military capability, threatens the mighty United States. None of this will matter to the wounded hawks, who know that Iranians are untrustworthy and bent on spreading their murderous influence. As President Bush reminded the West Point graduating class in 2002, "we are in a conflict between good and evil." Regime change in Iran is perhaps the most necessary step toward victory in the war against Islamo-fascism.

In the immediate aftermath of Iraq, therefore, the short-term risk of war with Iran will be higher than if no invasion had occurred. The nation will be hurting, licking its wounds, humiliated, and eager to restore its reputation. Although the threats it poses are rather minor, as we will discuss in future chapters, Iran may yet feel the rage of an angry, frustrated United States. No war is inevitable, of course. The American people certainly demonstrate no desire for a new war in the Middle East, just as they would not have supported another intervention in Southeast Asia in the 1970s. Still, the danger may be higher than most analysts realize, because of the way nations tend to react to defeat. While countries are in the anger stage, otherwise inexplicable events often occur. Just as a student should think twice before confronting a professor about a poor grade until he or she has passed into the acceptance stage, countries contemplating military action while in the throes of anger should be aware that their national interests probably would be better served by patience.

Overall, when our country loses, we all feel like losers. Since no one particularly likes to feel this way, before long we tend to convert the shame of defeat into anger, which is initially directed at our political and military leadership. Next, a treasonous minority within the country is often blamed, or the idea of country itself. People on the right, whose own personal identities typically are more tightly identified with their country, tend toward the former; those on the left, who identify less strongly with their country to begin with, the latter. In the final analysis, one thing is certain: The society suffers along with its individuals. The anger stage, though temporary, is the most dangerous, not only for minorities in our midst but for the state of the country itself.

## Stage 3: Depression

In 1974, retired Marine Lieutenant Colonel and economist William Corson conducted hundreds of interviews in an attempt to understand how people respond to military disasters like Vietnam. In his subsequent book, *The Consequences of Failure*, Corson argued that the "great silent majority" of Americans believe that their personal status is not only intertwined with their country's military prowess but also "dependent upon their support of the governing elite in its war-making decisions." Therefore, "one's attitude toward a nation at war is often grounded in one's attitude toward one's self."[45] War is something that we experience not only as a nation but also as individuals. In other words, many people take losing quite personally.

Victory is communal and must be shared, with parties and parades and public affirmations of our greatness. Defeat is personal, and is often suffered in isolation and silence. In the third stage of grief—depression—a population exhausted by anger turns inward, personalizing the disaster that has befallen its nation. The love of country can sometimes be nearly as strong as the love of family; we hate to see it fail in the same way we hate to see our children fail. And we react in much the same way.

Vietnam had very little measurable effect on the United States. There were no Viet Cong victory parades on the National Mall, no destruction of U.S. culture, and as we shall see in coming chapters, not even the loss of stature as a great power. To my knowledge, no American women or children were sold into slavery. But our team had lost to an underdog, and by extension, we all had lost. Nationwide depression was all but inevitable. By 1971, only one person in eight could not think of any way "in which life in the United States is getting worse."[46] President Jimmy Carter seemed to acknowledge that a "malaise" had fallen over the country in the 1970s, even though he didn't use the term. This presidential confirmation of the obvious was not well received, and only added to the nation's misery. Carter's position was a difficult one, though, for it is hard to govern a nation in the third postdefeat stage. Not until 1980 was the public ready to return to optimistic, hopeful leadership, which helps explain the appeal of Ronald Reagan's "Morning in America" message.

After Iraq, as with all four stages, individual reactions will vary widely during this overall period of national malaise. Some people—the rational ones—will not be affected by the defeat much at all. They will continue to live their lives exactly as before, without giving even a passing thought to Iraq. But many of us will find it difficult to deal with failure. During this third stage, after those deemed responsible for the debacle have been duly punished, we can expect to see further decreases in patriotism and political participation in the United States. It will continue to be difficult to take pride in being an American if that identity becomes associated with failure and defeat. This is of course not necessarily an ominous development—time and attention previously devoted to national concerns can often be more profitably spent on local or personal concerns. By separating themselves from the national disgrace, people will be able to find solace in other areas of their lives. This diversion of mental energy, along with the passage of time, will eventually help Americans to recover from their post-disaster malaise. Depression does not last forever.

The struggle over how we deal with Iraq will be in a sense an effort to redefine who we are as a people. Defeat will certainly test the mettle of this country, but one should have little doubt about the ultimate outcome. The United States is a strong nation, in many ways the strongest in the long history of the world, and it will eventually pass this test. In due time, it will pass on to the fourth and final stage after defeat.

## Stage 4: Acceptance—and Healing

Grief is temporary. Over time, most nations can recover from even the most devastating of disasters, both physically and psychologically. While in ancient times the vanquished could expect Carthage treatment—physical destruction and cultural annihilation—the modern era contains far more examples of gradual rejuvenation following defeat. Looking at Warsaw today, for example, one would not know that there was not one building standing in the city six decades ago.[47] Even Germany and Japan, similarly devastated by that war, now have healthy, functioning democracies and thriving economies. Once nations have moved past the painful initial stages, they can begin the more productive and healthy processes of acceptance, healing, and rebuilding.

In fact, such rejuvenation often leads to improvement over the prewar status quo. Many defeated societies emerge from defeat better off in a number of measurable categories than they were when the war began. Defeat can have a cleansing effect, inspiring the removal of the inefficient elements that contributed to national disgrace. Perhaps this can be seen as part of a process of political natural selection—in order to survive military disasters, societies need to adapt, or they die. Defeat exposes character, in both nations and teams. The strong learn during their period of suffering, and emerge even stronger for having gone through the process. The weak often find defeat impossible to deal with, and might not survive.

If defeat is to lead to improvement, countries must learn the right lessons and make the appropriate adjustments. Whereas victory can lead to complacency, defeat tends to concentrate the mind upon the need for innovation and reform. Between the world wars, Weimar Germany was far more motivated to absorb and learn the lessons of defeat than the Allies were of victory. As a consequence, the German economy (and, unfortunately, its war machine) was far more powerful and efficient by the end of the

1930s than were those of its neighbors. Defeat inspired widespread military innovation and progress, while the Allies became overconfident and enervated following their victory.

Obviously, not all examples are as ominous. Great Britain was far better off, both economically and politically, soon after the loss of its American colonies than it was prior to the Revolution.[48] Although the colonial war in Algeria toppled six French prime ministers and very nearly led to civil war, France experienced rapid economic and spiritual recovery in the decade that followed, which the most prominent historian of the era called "one of the miracles of the Western world, second only to Federal Germany's recovery after 1945." Out of the ashes of Algeria "arose an incomparably greater France than the world had seen for many a generation," demonstrating the essential strength of French society.[49]

Success can—and indeed usually does—rise from the ashes of defeat. But in order for it to do so, an important condition must be satisfied. Grief counselors and psychologists seem to be virtually unanimous about one thing: One of the most important parts of the process of healing is the acknowledgment of the reality of the loss.[50] As long as a society can continue to exist in denial of the existence of defeat, no meaningful recovery can begin. Thanks to the surprising early tactical success of the surge in Iraq, and the legend it created, it may prove difficult for the United States to move into this final stage of post-defeat development.

ACCEPTING DEFEAT

Unlike catastrophic defeats in major wars, when the presence of enemy troops in the capital leaves little doubt about who won and who lost, the endings of guerrilla wars are rarely uncontroversial. Although people may feel more comfortable with stark, unambiguous endings, reality does not always conform to our wishes. Vietnam at least had its dramatic end-of-the-war moment; Iraq, unfortunately, has no clear end in sight. In some ways it is unfortunate that we will never have that helicopters-leaving-the-embassy-roof image, much less a surrender-on-the-battleship scene following this war. As humiliating as those scenes were to the vanquished, they at least represented a clear end, a moment of "closure," to use the popular vernacular. Iraq has no such equivalent to North Vietnam to put an end to its tragic farce. It will continue to slowly bleed, as long as we are willing to stay, and beyond.

But even that helicopter moment proved to be too indecisive for some on the right, many of whom had convinced themselves that the Vietnam War had already been won by 1975. The primary lesson learned by the Nixon administration and its allies, from Kissinger to former Secretary of Defense Melvin Laird to the president himself, was not that the war was a mistake from the outset, but that within the Congress dwells a bottomless pit of perfidy.[51] Nixon maintained until the end of his life that the war in Vietnam was not in fact a loss for the United States. One of the chapters of his 1985 retrospective is titled "How We Won the War," which explains that his plan worked, only to be undercut by his political enemies.[52] Not everyone has fully acknowledged the U.S. defeat in Vietnam, which is part of the reason why it is still an open, festering wound. For some, the denial stage has never given way.

According to his book, Nixon made no mistakes over Vietnam during his time as president. In fact, if one were to rely solely on memoirs, it seems that very few leaders *ever* err, or at least have the courage to be honest about it afterwards. On the rare occasions that they do, they are often condemned by old enemies and allies alike. The experience of former Secretary of Defense Robert McNamara is the most prominent case in point. McNamara was of course one of the original architects of the war in Vietnam. He argued for escalation at many of its crucial early junctures, and was very influential in convincing President Johnson of the importance of victory. By the mid-1960s, he became so closely associated with the conflict that Vietnam was commonly referred to, fairly or unfairly, as "McNamara's War." "As much as any other individual," wrote one historian of the period, "McNamara personified the American commitment in Vietnam."[53]

As the war dragged on, however, McNamara grew despondent as he slowly came to the conclusion that it just could not be won. His tenure as secretary came to an end shortly after the Tet Offensive in 1968. Nearly a generation later, McNamara wrote that "I concede with painful candor and a heavy heart that . . . although we sought to do the right thing—and believed we were doing the right thing—in my judgment hindsight proves us wrong."[54] His confession of error, *In Retrospect*, is in many ways a remarkable book. McNamara admitted that the assumptions and fears he held that led him to support the war so strongly were baseless, and that he personally deserved much of the blame for its final outcome.

The book received nearly universal condemnation. Those on the left proved unwilling to forgive, or even to acknowledge the fact that McNamara was now admitting that they had been correct all along. The prominent Vietnam-era journalist David Halberstam was perhaps most blinded by residual rage, labeling

*In Retrospect* "a shallow, mechanistic, immensely disappointing book."[55] The *New York Times* opined that McNamara's "regret cannot be huge enough to balance the books for our dead soldiers. . . . What he took from them cannot be repaid by prime-time apology and stale tears, three decades later."[56] Hawks were no more sympathetic. Many on the right felt betrayed by McNamara, who seemed to be merely providing new ammunition to their longtime enemies. According to Colonel Harry Summers, a prominent right-wing Vietnam revisionist, McNamara's book proved that he was a "scoundrel" who was attempting to "curry favor with those who opposed the war."[57] McNamara had never been completely accepted in right-wing circles—his overbearingly arrogant management style had alienated too many people in and out of the Pentagon for him ever to have been a darling of the pro-war movement—but *In Retrospect* was the final insult. Overall, it is difficult to find anyone who lived through the era who has anything nice to say about McNamara's work. Its lessons, many of which could have been quite helpful to this country prior to the war in Iraq, were tragically lost amid the cacophony of rather petty criticism.

The uniform hostility that greeted *In Retrospect* will no doubt help to dissuade the architects of Iraq from making any such admissions of error, which is a shame indeed. Without such introspection, and admission of personal and strategic failure, the only thing that moves societies past military defeat is the passage of generations. Today, despite having had more than thirty years to think, research, and debate, America has reached no clear lessons from the Vietnam experience. For those who came of age afterward, the continuing anger can be hard to understand. But it is the nature of defeat to linger in our minds, and to haunt those who were involved with senses of horror, betrayal, and an often powerful desire for revenge. "The instinct for revenge is as elementary as thirst or sexual desire," noted Wolfgang Schivelbusch, and it is always present in some form after defeat.[58] Many people on all sides have never passed through the post-Vietnam anger stage, and have spent the better part of the past thirty years seeking some form of revenge. Indeed, the unsuccessful U.S. Supreme Court nominee Robert Bork spoke for all on left and right when he argued that no matter how much time passes after Vietnam, "healing will not happen until the people who remember have passed from this world."[59] One should perhaps be equally pessimistic about the prospects for post-Iraq reconciliation, at least until all those involved either admit failure or have too passed from this world.

The United States is not likely to pass through the four stages of grief until it comes to grips with the reality of defeat in Iraq. If history can be considered a guide to the future, certain segments of this society are unlikely ever to accept the notion that the war was a failure. As was the case following Vietnam, the leaders who brought us into Iraq will no doubt lead the charge of denial. At the very least, those on the far right will argue that the United States was never technically beaten by any foe; instead, they will argue, we defeated ourselves. A debate will emerge over what really happened in Iraq, one that is going to look a great deal like the one that has raged since Vietnam. And if it follows the Vietnam precedent, nothing of importance will ever be settled.

The only real effect of the arguments over the outcome of Iraq will be to prevent, or at least delay, any large-scale, meaningful recovery from the debacle.

# Double or Nothing

Barbara Tuchman's observation that "to admit error and cut losses is rare among individuals, unknown among states" applies with equal power to the twenty-first as to the fourteenth century.[60] Instead of accepting defeat, which is a necessary step toward healing, countries are much more likely to do the opposite. Loss-averse leaders seem to become desperate in the face of disaster, ignore rational calculations of odds, and take gambles that appear to hold hope, no matter how slim, of turning the tide.[61] In Iraq, the so-called surge was equal parts strategic adjustment and desperate gamble. Losing wars gracefully seems to be a near impossibility for most leaders. Cutting losses and moving on, although common enough in everyday life, is always an agonizingly difficult decision for any government to reach, even after a prolonged, expensive, and manifestly unsuccessful war.[62]

In every war there comes a point when giving up makes a lot more sense than continuing to fight. Wars are fought in the pursuit of specific foreign policy goals, not to test the mettle of our great nation against that of a foe. When those goals are no longer achievable, or when they are deemed fundamentally unimportant, the war should be ended, no matter what the psychological cost may be. While hawks may commonly accuse Iraq war opponents of being "invested in defeat," in reality it is they who are invested in victory for *victory's* sake, not for *America's*. As we shall see in the chapters that follow, it is hard to imagine how any victory in Iraq would serve the national interest. The desire to press on at all costs, never give up, is no longer driven by national interest but by our desire to avoid losing. Victory for victory's sake alone is not worth having.

IN ORDER FOR the recovery to begin, the war must end. It is therefore better for America to end it sooner rather than later, to give the healing process a chance to start. A decisive admission of failure would be far more helpful in the long run to American society than the continued misguided effort to achieve what could not help but be a pointless, Pyrrhic victory. Although politically dangerous for any leader, an admission of failure would be psychologically helpful for the nation at large.

Often a change in government is necessary before there can be a fundamental redefinition of wartime goals and commitments.[63] Perhaps a future American leader will prove to be courageous enough to end the madness in Iraq, and end it decisively. Only a clear break with the policies of the Bush administration has the potential to minimize the ambiguity, the acrimony, and the suffering of the Iraq Syndrome, and put America on a faster road toward recovery.

It is probably too soon to speak of forgiveness. The issue will be too raw, and the nation too angry, to move past the initial stages of post-defeat development for some time. Partisan rancor is likely to be a central feature of American politics for at least the next few presidential administrations. But if this country is to move past Iraq, it will need to put that anger aside. Yes, the war was a catastrophic mistake, one that led to tens of thousands of unnecessary deaths. Yes, as it turns out, Saddam had no super-weapons and no connection to 9/11. But what is done cannot be undone. Those waiting for (or demanding) neoconservative apologies or admissions of error are likely to be waiting a long time. As Robert McNamara found out, the reality of postwar national trauma means that there is little to be gained by being intellectually honest.

No personal or national reaction to defeat is inevitable. In fact, the most dire of the predictable reactions to Iraq are within our ability to control. Through a recognition of our likely reactions, and the stages we will probably go through together as a people, we can control if not overcome them completely. Perhaps we can also channel their energy in more productive directions.

The next few chapters will deal with more specific outcomes of the war, attempting to separate the likely from the unlikely on the home front, for U.S. security, and for Iraq and the Middle East. The national security consequences of Iraq will be trivial; our national self-image, however, is going to take some time to recover as we travel through the post-disaster stages toward eventual acceptance. Higher levels of pessimism and depression are likely to be staples of the next few years, since neither individuals nor states can tolerate being thought of as "losers." And unlike sports, we can't simply wait for the chance at redemption that "next season" will bring.

# 2

## The Iraq Syndrome

### DISASTER AND THE HOME FRONT

T HERE IS NO SHORTAGE of writing about defeat. We know a great deal about why armies have lost, and excruciating detail about how. We know what mistakes the generals made on the battlefield, or the politicians behind the scenes, from ancient times through to the twenty-first century. We are all too familiar with the bad luck and the hubris (and occasionally the enemy's heroism) that have made defeat a foregone conclusion. How war is lost is no real mystery.

What comes afterward, on the other hand, is much less familiar. People don't seem to be too interested in the losers, in what happens to the vanquished. Our heroes are nearly always the winners, especially those who overcome great odds to achieve victory. We follow their exploits, and pass down their tales of glory to future generations. The defeated, however, are left to fend for themselves, in anonymous ignominy. "The effects of defeat," notes the historian Michael Geyer, "have, with rare exceptions, not been the subject of historical inquiry."[1] History is not only written *by* the victors, it is written *about* the victors as well. This is rather odd, really, because defeat often has greater historical importance than victory. Losing wars, even small wars, commonly affects societies to a much greater extent than does winning. Defeat serves society as breeze does a fire, extinguishing the weak and fueling the strong.

In 2007, many Americans seemed to enter the second phase of post-disaster development. Poll after poll revealed that the typical American "can-do" optimism was largely absent in many segments of society, as majorities in both parties reported feeling that the country was heading in the wrong direction. Anger at, and lack of confidence in, all branches of the government was at historic highs. The overwhelming majority of Americans reported general dissatisfaction with "the way things are going" in the United States.[2] The war in Iraq drove anger and resentment in virtually every segment of the American body politic.

What will happen to this country as it moves through the predictable stages of post-disaster development? Many analysts seem to feel that the United States stands at the beginning of a new era, one that will be less predicable, more dangerous, and essentially chaotic. While no functioning crystal balls exist, history contains enough examples of upset defeats to allow us to speculate with some confidence about what the immediate future is likely to bring. There is certainly no shortage of precedent. Although the experience of defeat is never the same twice, there are enough common features to help us anticipate coming events on the home front in the years immediately following Iraq, as the American people travel down the road, with luck, to ultimate acceptance.

First, there is bad news: The brunt of the war's consequences are probably going to be felt on the home front. Because of how people typically react to the prospect of losing, Iraq is likely to affect negatively the politics, economy, and society of the United States beyond what any reasonable rational calculation would predict. The psychological impact of this disaster will far outweigh the empirical. The good news, however, is that the actual measurable consequences will probably be fairly minimal. Iraq will not lead to major convulsions in international politics, nor will it spell the end of American influence around the globe. War is not likely to spread across the Persian Gulf, much less beyond. Levels of terrorism will not skyrocket. Visions of cataclysm might sell newspapers, but that does not mean that they are particularly likely. After Iraq, the world will probably look much the same as it did before. Calm will eventually return, and before long it will appear as if the war never occurred.

That story will have to wait until the next chapter. Domestically, as we will see, the worst may be yet to come.

## Politics

Nowhere will the effects of the Iraq disaster be more apparent than in American politics. Four major trends will probably dominate the postwar era: high levels of partisanship, marked by rancor, bitterness, and decreased levels of compromise; a reassertion of the power of the legislative branch at the expense of the executive, at least in the short term; generalized anger at the institutions of government, as much as at the individuals who run them; and an eventual reassertion of the right wing as America emerges from the initial, more pernicious stages of post-defeat development.

## PARTISANSHIP IN DOMESTIC AND FOREIGN POLICY

In general, one should be careful of putting too much credence in the "red state/blue state" metaphor that is so popular with the media these days. No matter what happens in Iraq, it will always be true that much more unites Americans than divides them. The illusion of a deeply divided America is a reflection of our political system, which tends to reward candidates who stake out positions on the fringes of the spectrum. The parties today are far more polarized and antagonistic than the country at large, and there is certainly more partisanship in Washington than in the hinterlands.[3] The United States is a fundamentally strong, mostly unified society, one that is unlikely to be torn asunder by the experience of defeat.

Still, there are many issues that do divide the opinion of the public. Not least of these is the war, of course, and relative levels of partisan anger are likely to rise in its wake. Iraq has already destroyed the unprecedented unity that the country experienced after the 9/11 terrorist attacks and raised fighting between the parties to levels higher than at any time in modern history. Not even the contentious Vietnam era saw the kind of division in the American electorate over the wisdom of beginning and continuing a foreign policy action.[4] The next few election cycles will probably be some of the most bitter in recent memory, as leaders of both parties feel pressure from their highly mobilized, emotional bases to remain steadfast and avoid any hint of capitulation or compromise. This passion, driven in part by fear, guilt, and mutual recrimination, will lead to increased partisanship and concomitant political paralysis.

The pattern is quite common among countries in the anger and depression stages after defeat, as people seek outlets for their rage.

Disputes over the basic meaning of the war will probably continue for at least a generation, if not more. Was the invasion a necessary response to pressing post-9/11 security threats? A grand, noble effort to bring democracy and freedom to the Middle East? A spectacularly misguided strategic and moral disaster? Consensus will be rare in this period, with opinions divided along preexisting fault lines of party identification. Indeed, the war can be thought of as an earthquake that will deepen and widen the fissures already existing in the crust of American politics. American society may be more united in the deeper levels—to continue the awkward geology metaphor, in the mantle—but on the surface, in the crust, fault lines are visible and the potential for divisive shocks is ever present.

Consider what happened to U.S. politics in the aftermath of Vietnam. As we saw in the previous chapter, the war remains an open wound for Americans over fifty. It was the most important event in the political development of an entire generation, the first lesson many baby boomers learned about international politics. The bitter recriminations it spawned spilled over from foreign policy into domestic, helping to bring down two presidents and poison American politics for decades to come. The specter of Vietnam has hung over every presidential election involving candidates from that generation. Conservative ire toward Bill Clinton, for instance, was founded on the perception that he was a part of the radical left during Vietnam. In their minds he became intimately connected with the protest movement, those who not only avoided military service but actively undermined the U.S. war effort. The photos of Clinton with long hair at Oxford in the late sixties were to some people the moral equivalent of traveling to Hanoi with Jane Fonda. John Kerry was even worse, a traitor to the pro-war cause, a McNamaraesque turncoat who served in Vietnam only to return to support the radicals. People can only forgive a certain level of questionable decisions made by rich young playboys. At least George W. Bush, whose wealth and connections allowed him to avoid the war, did not actively support the other side.

The United States emerged from Vietnam far more divided than when it went in. During the Johnson administration, a majority of Republicans were opposed to the war, while Democrats were generally supportive and optimistic. When Richard Nixon took office in 1969, these positions reversed: Suddenly Democrats reported believing that Vietnam was a mistake, while Republicans tended to believe that the war would soon be over and that the peace talks were progressing.[5] Party identification, rather than national interest, became the decisive determinant of foreign policy belief for many people. This phenomenon is still very much visible today, since Republicans are much more likely to believe that going to war in Iraq was the correct decision (still), and that it is going well, than are Democrats.

In foreign policy, Vietnam marked the end of what scholars often refer to as a period of broad national consensus.[6] Prior to the war, it was sometimes said that "politics stops at the water's edge," which meant that while the nation might have been divided on domestic issues, when it came to foreign affairs it generally spoke with one voice. Although that ideal was never quite achieved in practice, it is true that from World War II until the 1960s, divisions among Americans over questions of foreign policy did not fall neatly along partisan lines.[7] Despite their differences, both political parties tended to view the world through a similar, centrist lens. This prewar consensus had been based on a common appraisal of national interests in the face of the growing Communist threat, and our leaders generally viewed the world through the lenses of *realpolitik*. The war in Vietnam gave rise to extremes on the far left and far right in foreign policy analysis, both of which had major disagreements with the realists. Radicals of both stripes had always existed in American discourse, but they had mostly operated on the periphery prior to Vietnam. Defeat proved to be a powerful centrifugal force, which spun people (and political power) out to the edges of foreign policy at the expense of the realist center. The war in Iraq would probably never have occurred, in fact, had that consensus not frayed in the aftermath of the Vietnam disaster.

Throughout the 1950s and 1960s, *realpolitik* was the dominant intellectual paradigm for scholars and practitioners of U.S. foreign policy, and its appeal crossed party lines. But the realists did not win every battle. In fact, the most prominent realist thinkers in the 1960s, like George Kennan, Walter Lippmann, Hans Morgenthau, and Kenneth Waltz, strongly opposed the war in Vietnam.[8] To these men, such intervention would only have been worthwhile if it had the potential to affect the balance of power between the Soviet Union and the West in a favorable way. Moralistic crusades to prevent the spread of communism to isolated, resource-poor corners of the globe made little sense. Realists were also virtually unanimous in opposition to the war in Iraq, since they did not see the wisdom in a quixotic effort to bring democracy and freedom to the Middle East by force.[9] No matter what kind of government was in charge of Iraq, realists argued, the country was likely to be suspicious of Iran and hostile to the United States. In addition, Iraqi nationalists would be likely to resist conquest and occupation. Both times, unfortunately, their counsel was ignored.

Following Vietnam, many people broke away from the realist center into one of two relatively new intellectual paths. First and most obviously, the far left was given a big boost by the war. Since Vietnam was part of a political maturation process for the post–World War II generation, many young people proved to be especially susceptible to the arguments of left-wing intellectuals such as the linguist Noam Chomsky and the historians Howard Zinn and Gabriel Kolko, who flipped the conventional moral calculus of the Cold War on its head. It was the United States, not the Soviet Union, that was the evil empire responsible for superpower tensions, this new generation was told. Those on the radical left not only condemned the actions of the United States, but often actively sang the virtues of the Viet Cong and North Vietnam, as if they were merely benevolent, oppressed innocents. The rather obvious pointlessness and savagery of the Vietnam War convinced many baby boomers that the United States and capitalism were indeed inherently hypocritical, unjust, even evil.

Another intellectual tradition rose out of Vietnam's ashes, one that was in large part a reaction to the rise of the radical left. Modern neoconservatism emerged in the 1970s, initially to answer the anti-Americanism of the anti-war movement, and then in response to what it saw as the moral relativism of Nixon and détente. According to these members of the far right, communism was an evil force that had to be combated and rolled back, not merely contained. Peaceful co-existence with the Communist world should never have been considered. A number of these hawkish analysts disagreed with the emerging conventional wisdom about Vietnam, which held that the war had been a mistake from the beginning. Prominent members of the right, like Norman Podhoretz of *Commentary* magazine, General William Westmoreland, and California governor Ronald Reagan, made the argument that the war had been a just, moral crusade, a poorly executed but noble battle in the larger war against communism. In fact, "we have never fought in a more moral cause," argued Nixon.[10] Neoconservatives, many of whom were converts from liberalism (hence the "neo" in neocon), over-corrected for the transgressions of the "blame America first" crowd, as former U.S. Ambassador to the United Nations Jeane Kirkpatrick famously called the far left, asserting that the United States was not only on the side of goodness during the Cold War but in fact could do no wrong. To suggest otherwise was not only patriotically incorrect but borderline treasonous. Today, Communists may have been replaced by Islamic fundamentalists, but the message from the far right remains the same: The United States is the world's good guy, struggling against the forces of evil that lurk around every corner.

To those who remained in the realist center, the far left and the far right had much in common, and still do.[11] Most obviously, both extremes consider international politics to be an eternal struggle between good and evil. To those on the far left, the ruling classes still have to be opposed and defeated; on the far right, "Islamo-fascism" has replaced communism as the main enemy of freedom. Both are evidence of what the political scientist Kenneth Boulding once called "cowboy theories" of international relations, which see the world as a contest between the good guys in the white hats and the bad guys in the black hats.[12] It should perhaps go without saying that President Bush sees himself as a cowboy in a white hat, leading the charge against evil in our time.

Realists are generally skeptical about moral crusades against evil, whether the black hats be worn by Communists, capitalists, or Islamic fundamentalists. Classical *realpolitik* suggests that there are no inherently good or inherently evil countries, and that such calculations are entirely dependent upon where one sits. All states tend to act in similar ways, and more or less rationally, defending what they see as their interests. According to the realists, the United States like any country is bound to have rivals and enemies, but it should not fall into the trap of thinking that it is on a crusade against the forces of darkness. All people, and all countries, are motivated by forces that are basically the same. To the critics of realism on the right and left, both of whom were given a major boost by Vietnam, this thinking seemed like heretical, cowardly moral relativism.

Today, both the far left and the far right are still quite visible and active in American politics. The left is perhaps most prominently represented by the "moveon.org" anti-war movement and its various Nader-inspired critiques of U.S. foreign policy. Members of the far right have been far more directly influential, earning important roles in the Bush administration, especially in the offices of the vice president and secretary of defense. After 9/11, the neoconservatives were able to out-debate the administration's realists in the State Department about the wisdom and potential for success of an attempt to spread democracy to Iraq. Our naive president found the far right members of his cabinet to be convincing, and launched his crusade against evil, which has led us into the current mess.

Were it not for Vietnam, therefore, we would have no neocon-servatives, and no war in Iraq. Overall, the war left a far more bitter, more polarized, and less thoughtful America in its wake. Ironically, the political scientists Ole Holsti and James Rosenau were to note a decade later, "an American effort to prevent the unification by force of Vietnam ended in a unified Vietnam and a disunited United States."[13] If we are not careful, Iraq could do the same. Defeat can have sometimes long-lasting, unforeseeable consequences.

## THE RISE OF LEGISLATIVE POWER

The political battles that lie ahead will not merely pit the par-ties against one another. The Iraq disaster will probably lead to increased tension between the branches, as the legislature reas-serts its role in the execution of foreign policy after perceived executive overreach and/or incompetence. Over the course of the next few years, we are likely to see a far more assertive Congress, one that will clash repeatedly with the White House. And the public is likely to be broadly supportive of its efforts.

The Bush administration took advantage of a compliant, friendly, post-9/11 Congress to expand the power of the execu-tive to unprecedented levels. Vice President Cheney, who after all was a product of the Watergate era when he served as President Ford's chief of staff, made it a priority to reassert the power of the presidency to levels he thought appropriate. Following Cheney's lead, the administration seemed to hold the view that Congress "works *for* us, not *with* us," as the longtime presidential adviser David Gergen told PBS's *Frontline*, and that the executive was "the lead branch not a co-equal branch."[14] On both large constitutional issues (domestic surveillance, signing statements, Guantánamo Bay) and rather absurdly picayune issues of stubborn principle (who advises task forces, how many people are on his staff, etc.), the vice president has led the charge to reestablish what Arthur M. Schlesinger, Jr., once called the "imperial presidency."[15] Because of the rather remarkable deference, or perhaps cowardice, on Capitol Hill following 9/11, the office of the president is more powerful than it has been in decades.

Cheney also apparently felt that the extreme secrecy of the Nixon administration set a precedent worthy of repetition. The vice president has sought to keep all his actions, including where he actually is at any given moment, a state secret. The rest of the Bush administration seems to have followed his lead. Nixonesque secrecy might have helped the White House execute its policies, but it has once again proven to be a public relations disaster. Whoever succeeds the Bush administration can expect to experience a backlash from a public tired of being kept in the dark about the activities of its government. Since secrecy is in many ways the enemy of democracy, this trend should not be unwelcome.

A similar process occurred· as the war in Vietnam drew to a conclusion. The legislative branch, which had been compliant and cooperative with executive wishes throughout the early stages of the war, began to reassert itself in the early 1970s. By the end of the decade, congressional oversight had been reasserted over covert operations, intelligence collection, foreign aid, confirmation of officials, national emergencies, and funding.[16] In general, Congress made it far more difficult for the executive branch to govern with impunity, out of the spotlight and away from the public eye. Checks and balances had been reestablished, for better or for worse. Vice President Cheney's attempt to bring back the rules of the game that existed in the Nixonian good old days is rather bizarre, therefore, because those days were fairly short-lived.

Nowhere was the fighting between the branches more intense than over the power to make war. In an ideal world, U.S. foreign policy would be a balance combining the best of both branches; in reality, of course, it is a constant struggle, one in which the imperatives of party too often outweigh those of the nation. Both the executive and the legislative seem to have a compelling constitutional argument for why they should take the lead in deciding when and where the United States fights. Article II of the Constitution makes it clear that the president is the commander in chief of the armed forces of the United States, but Article I (and the sequence is not an accident) gives the Congress the power to declare war. What exactly the founding fathers meant by that apparent contradiction has been the subject of two hundred years of rather indecisive debate, one which was re-engaged following Vietnam.[17]

Although the Congress had passed what became known as the "Gulf of Tonkin Resolution" in 1964 authorizing the president to "take all necessary steps, including the use of armed force," to assist U.S. allies in Southeast Asia, there never was a formal declaration of war for Vietnam.[18] In fact, the Congress has only declared war five times—prior to the War of 1812, the Mexican-American War in 1846, the Spanish-American War in 1898, and the two world wars—but of course the United States has used force almost continually throughout its history. All of the other military deployments, both big and small, were executed without formal declarations. In matters of war, Congress has traditionally deferred to the president. As Vietnam dragged on, however, many lawmakers, reflecting the general mood of the country, decided that the executive branch had abused its power to execute the war, and that deference came to an end.

In November 1973, both Houses passed what became known as the War Powers Act and sustained it over President Nixon's veto. The new law required the president to notify the Congress within forty-eight hours of a deployment of U.S. forces overseas, and remove them within ninety days without explicit congressional authorization to continue. On the surface, this seemed to address a dilemma at the center of the debate about the power to make war, which has always been the tension between *efficiency* and *democracy*. The executive branch can make decisions swiftly and it houses far more expertise in foreign affairs, but it is through the legislature that the people can more directly affect the process. The War Powers Act attempted to address this problem, and allow both efficiency and democratic oversight in warmaking, by granting the president the power to order U.S. troops into harm's way abroad for three months without congressional permission. This would presumably allow the White House to address immediately the urgent crises that arise, while limiting its power to sustain a war without the consent of the legislative branch, and by extension the people of the United States.

President Nixon never acknowledged the law, claiming that it conflicted with his constitutional power as commander in chief. In fact, no president has ever taken steps that could be interpreted as supportive of the War Powers Act, and all have proceeded instead as if the act did not exist. The wars in Iraq, plus the deployments in Lebanon, Grenada, Haiti, Kosovo, and elsewhere, were fought by an executive branch unencumbered by pesky legislative interference. Presidents occasionally consult the Congress for symbolic resolutions, but very rarely do they ask for formal declarations of war as clearly required by the U.S. Constitution.

Those who remember their basic civics classes might think that the power to make war might be an issue for the Supreme Court to decide. After all, it is a question of constitutional interpretation, one that explicitly pits one branch against another. The Supreme Court has indeed ruled consistently on this matter: It has determined that this is in fact not a constitutional matter at all, but a political question. In other words, it does not pit the executive vs. the legislative branch as much as it does the Republican Party vs. the Democratic Party. Since the Court typically stays out of political questions, it has refused even to hear a case about the constitutionality of the War Powers Act.

Evidently the justices are able to maintain this line of reasoning while keeping a straight face, which is no small feat in itself. Surely there are very few more important constitutional questions than the ones governing war. The failure of the Supreme Court to consider the War Powers Act is a mind-boggling, irresponsible abdication of its most basic responsibility as final arbiter of constitutional questions. And it undermines the democratic process, in essence granting the executive branch free rein to make war whenever and wherever it pleases.

There is little doubt that the Constitution puts the president in charge of the nation's military, but that it does not give him (or her) the right to determine when it is used. That power ought to be in the hands of the people, through the Congress. No president should have the power to make war by himself—this is what separates democracies from dictatorships, and what should make the United States different from, say, Saddam Hussein's Iraq. When one person alone makes all the important decisions regarding war and peace, the nation runs the risk of being led into ill-advised adventures by inexperienced politicians more adept at campaigning than running a foreign policy.

Think of it this way: The commander of a brigade has the ability to make most of the important decisions regarding how his troops fight. He cannot, however, determine when and why they fight, which are decisions made above. Similarly, the commander in chief can determine the strategy during wartime, or *how* the nation fights, but he or she cannot decide when and why wars begin. In a democracy, those decisions are made above, by the people. In the U.S. system, of course, the Congress is the most direct representative of the people. For all its flaws, the Congress ought to have power over when and where this country goes to war. The War Powers Act deserves to be the recognized law of the land.

Overall, the next few presidents are likely to face strong opposition from a reassertive Congress, in war powers and other areas. By the close of 2007, there were signs that congressional deference was already beginning to come to a conclusion. "What you have seen," observed Senator Lindsey Graham (R-SC), "is a Congress, which has been AWOL through intimidation or lack of unity, get off the sidelines and jump in with both feet."[19] As the Bush administration recedes into history, the pendulum of federal power is likely to continue its swing toward the legislative branch at the expense of the White House. The debacle in Iraq may well provide the spark for a shift in public opinion toward the reining in of this new version of the imperial presidency.

If one has faith in democracy, in the basic idea that the people know best, the reassertion of the legislative power, which is highly likely in the wake of Iraq, should be a welcome development. After all, a balance between branches is clearly what the founders intended for their new nation. An unchecked executive branch should be a frightening prospect not only for members of the party out of power. Furthermore, in the few periods where the Congress has flexed its muscles in foreign affairs, the United States has been more restrained in its foreign adventures. As future chapters will show, such a change would be quite a relief for this country following Iraq.

## ANGER AT INSTITUTIONS

In his study of post-Vietnam America, William Corson argued that trust in government, which had always been strong among the American people, had been replaced by cynicism. "The public wonders," he wrote, "how it can support a government that is either incredibly unrealistic, inept, or hypocritical—or all three."[20] A similar process is occurring right now. The next president is virtually guaranteed a contentious, unpopular, and probably brief tenure in the White House. The fact that Nixon did not start the war in Vietnam mattered little to an angry nation. He was held just as responsible in their eyes, *ex officio*.

Trust in the institutions of government will also probably drop precipitously, if temporarily, because of the failure in Iraq. Presidential approval ratings were at historic lows throughout 2007, but those of Congress stood even lower.[21] The American people seemed to hold the institutions of government responsible for this tragedy as well as the individual leaders who made the crucial decisions. It would not be the first time that they did so; with luck, perhaps it can be the last.

Public trust in government plummeted steadily as the Johnson administration sunk America deeper into the Vietnam quagmire, and the trend continued throughout the Nixon era. According to polling data from the period, general levels of happiness also fell to all-time low levels. This phenomenon was not contained to merely the discontented baby boomer set: all levels of American society, regardless of race, age, region, level of education and income, reported feeling less satisfied with both their government and their lives after Vietnam. Happiness rebounded more rapidly than trust. Polls in 1978 suggest that Americans may have been happier than in 1971, but they still distrusted their government. As with the earlier polls, it was not just "disgruntled old people or dissatisfied metropolitan dwellers or hard-to-please college graduates" who doubted the intentions and the statements of their government, according to the social psychologist Angus Campbell. "It was everywhere."[22]

With the prevailing anger at institutions and likely shift of power toward the Congress, it is a wonder that anyone would want to take over the reins in 2008. Unless the next president begins the process of withdrawal from Iraq immediately after taking office, in order to give the country a chance to move on to the later stages of recovery by 2012, he or she is likely to be removed by a discontented public after one term. Smart political operatives might just want the other side to win this one. Control of the

White House in 2008, while a short-term asset, might turn out to be a long-term political liability.

## THE RISE OF THE RIGHT

Finally, it is worth noting that as nations begin to recover from the initial stages of defeat, they often find solace in patriotism, renewed nationalism, and right-wing politics. People can only feel bad about their country (and by extension themselves) for so long. Eventually, leaders rise who convince the public that it is acceptable to take pride in their heritage and in their country once again. They usually find that the masses are willing, and indeed eager, to put the experience of war behind them and listen to the patriotic messages from representatives of the right.

The bigger the disaster, the more the right tends to benefit. Post–World War I Germany is the most obvious example of a nation lurching to the right in the ashes of defeat, but it is hardly the only one. Conservative rule soon returned to England following the loss of the colonies. Ronald Reagan's popularity would be inexplicable without the Vietnam-fueled malaise that preceded his presidency. The Gipper was among the first of the revisionists to argue that the United States had not, in fact, lost the war in Vietnam. "Well, the truth of the matter is that we did have victory," said the governor and presidential candidate. "We continue to talk about losing that war. We didn't lose that war. We won virtually every engagement."[23] Reagan dealt with the Vietnam Syndrome by denying that it had any right to exist. The people proved more than willing to go along.

The rise of the political right is by no means an inevitable outcome. After all, it is hard to make a case that the right wing in either Germany or Japan has been able to attract much support in the six decades since World War II. But it is at least quite possible that the United States will experience a strengthening of its right wing as part of its post-Iraq development, in the medium term, as the country struggles through the four stages of defeat. For some, this will of course be a welcome, overdue development, and light at the end of the tunnel; for others, it will be yet another reason to believe that the war was a disaster for this country.

The Vietnam War helped to bring down two presidencies, deepened political divisions, and tilted the balance of constitutional power back to the legislative branch. It strengthened the case of those who blame America for all that is wrong in the world, and gave rise to others who refuse to blame America for anything. Despite repeated announcements that its effects are behind us, few Americans who lived through that troubled era seem to have been able to put its passions to rest. They are there, lurking under the surface, ever ready to explode anew with full force. Only time will tell whether Iraq turns out to have the same effect.

## Economics

Despite the suspicions of various Marxists and conspiracy theorists, modern countries rarely go to war in order to get rich. Although there are clearly segments of modern economies that benefit from wartime spending, the common left-wing contention that a "military-industrial complex" drives the United States into wars ignores, or perhaps just misunderstands, a fundamental fact about the economics of war: While a relatively short burst of increased spending can provide a boost in the short term, over the long haul war tends to be a drag on economic performance.[24] Only profoundly irrational governments would go to war in order to enrich certain limited sectors of their societies at the expense of all others. Fairly or unfairly, leaders are held responsible for the economic performance of their nations. No amount of help from corporate allies in the military-industrial complex can rescue a politician if the overall economy is harmed by the war. And war often hurts growth far more that it helps.

Even seemingly strong economies can be severely damaged by war. The great Spanish Empire was the envy of the world before its back was broken by the eighty-year misadventure in the Low Countries. The Soviet economy proved unable to bear the costs imposed by the war in Afghanistan. Vietnam was the primary cause of the inflationary spiral that led the United States into high levels of unemployment, low or even negative growth rates, and a weak dollar throughout the 1970s.[25] The war led to the era of "stagflation" and the worst recession since the 1930s. It was during the seventies that economists developed the so-called Misery Index, which was more useful as a symbol of the era than as an economic indicator. The index was a simple addition of the unemployment rate to the inflation rate, and it has never been higher than it was during the Ford, Carter, and first Reagan administrations.

The economic consequences of Iraq are hard to forecast, in part because the war has been almost unique in two aspects. One of these atypical features is positive, at least in the short term: The war has not been accompanied by much measurable inflation. The increased spending that governments must undertake to pay for wars has in the past usually resulted in a certain amount of inflation. Although it is sometimes said that "inflation and war are eternal partners," through the first five years of Iraq rates remained low.[26] Were the war to drag on for a decade, of course, this may well change. It is not clear that inflationary pressures can be held at bay in perpetuity.

The second difference between this war and those that have preceded it is somewhat more ominous: Unlike the first Gulf War, which was financed largely by our Coalition partners, the second war with Iraq was fought *entirely* with borrowed money. Previous wars have been financed with a combination of borrowing, such as the war bonds of World War II fame, and war taxes. Large tax increases in 1951 and again in 1952 helped offset the costs of the Korean War. President Johnson, afraid to risk congressional support for his Great Society programs, asked for only a relatively modest package of tax increases to pay for Vietnam. Although this was still more than what the Bush administration has done to pay for Iraq, most economists today believe that the taxes Johnson asked for were insufficient to protect the country from inflation.[27]

At least partially because they assumed that the war would be a cakewalk, Bush administration officials made no serious plans to pay for it. They certainly never asked the American people to make fiscal sacrifices to help defray the costs of war. Even as it became clear that these costs were going to be far higher than originally thought, and that Iraqi oil was not going be able to foot the bill, the administration decided that the short-term political costs that would be incurred by new taxes outweighed the damage to long-term economic health that fighting a war with borrowed money would do. The United States did not feel the true economic impact of the war because it essentially put the whole thing on a credit card. Eventually, the bills will come due.

By the end of 2007, three decades of irresponsible spending had saddled the United States with a debt of approximately $9 trillion, or around $30,000 for each person in the country. The total federal budget was around $2.8 trillion; in fiscal year 2007, the United States devoted almost $244 billion of that, or 13.4 percent, to interest on the debt. The debt is constantly growing, of course, since our leaders add hundreds of billions to it every year. By its end, the war in Iraq will have cost at least $3 trillion, if the Nobel Prize–winning economist Joseph Stiglitz is correct, and all of it will be simply thrown onto our huge pile of IOUs.[28] The United States, once the world's largest creditor and its "economic engine," has become its largest debtor, and there is no end in sight.

Potentially more disturbing is the attitude of our leaders toward what would seem to be a rather serious fiscal problem. Governments throughout history have taken years to pay off the debts incurred in war. There is no telling when the money borrowed for this war will be paid back, however, since apparently public debt has somehow ceased to be a problem. As Vice President Cheney told Treasury Secretary Paul O'Neill, "Reagan proved deficits don't matter."[29] Never mind that the Treasury secretary is supposed to be the administration's lead official on economic matters; evidently, the vice president's hear-no-evil, see-no-evil approach to deficits and debt was all that this country needed. Cheney's economic logic was as sound as his strategic. Overall, there is simply no evidence whatsoever that anyone in either party is making any plan to pay the borrowed money back.

When surpluses arise, tax cuts or increased spending have been in the offing, as if the debt did not exist. This money we as a society owe has simply become part of the background noise of the U.S. economic policy. Someday, probably sooner rather than later, this might just start making our creditors a bit nervous.

It is little wonder that the Bush administration decided that the staggering amounts of debt simply did not matter, since they will be long gone by the time that the interest payments become truly crippling to the U.S. economy. It will be a problem for future generations to worry about. Perhaps our grandchildren will be able to figure out a way to pay for this war; or perhaps they will simply follow the lead of their elders and pass it on to *their* kids. Making minimum monthly payments on rapidly growing debt is apparently the American way.

OIL

There is at least one way in which the American people are beginning to feel the cost of the war. As everyone who has taken a trip abroad in the last five years knows, the dollar has taken an enormous beating while this war has raged. Since 2002, its value has fallen about 30 percent against an index of major currencies.[30] The weakness in the dollar, which is in large part a reflection of the market's unease with the state of the U.S. economy, does more then merely hurt our would-be tourists. It has helped drive oil, which is still traded exclusively in dollars, to costs never before seen.

The day that the war started, March 20, 2003, was hectic for commodity traders. Investors were nervous, and their anxiety drove the price of oil up over thirty dollars a barrel before it finished the day at $28.61. Traders told *New York Times* reporters that they expected the price to settle "at $25 to $32 during—and perhaps after—the war."[31] That prediction, as it turns out, was a bit optimistic. In May 2008, the price of a barrel of crude oil broke $120 for the first time. Worldwide demand rose during those intervening five years, to be sure, but it hardly quadrupled. The remarkable rise in the price of oil is directly related to the war, which helped to weaken the dollar and caused serious instability in the market.

Oil is traded on the futures market, which means that its price today is in part a reflection of what investors think it will be worth tomorrow. The insecurity that the war has brought has both discouraged exploration for new supplies in the Middle East and added a "security premium" onto every barrel bought and sold. If there had been no invasion of Iraq, the price would more accurately reflect the forces of supply and demand, and would probably be about half of what it is today.

The implications of expensive oil for the global economy are likely to be profound. Petroleum-producing states, many of which are not the world's most democratic or friendly to U.S. interests, are making more money than ever before. The war has been a godsend for Iran, Russia, Saudi Arabia, and Venezuela. For consuming nations, however, the news is grim. Historically speaking, U.S. economic performance has always been inversely related to the price of oil. As prices rise, productivity and growth fall.[32] When prices are low, like in the mid-to-late 1990s, the U.S. economy expands. The next few years are likely to be very difficult economic times for the United States.

Americans may soon look back on the days when they were paying $3.50 for a gallon of gasoline with nostalgic fondness, because all projections have the price rising steadily over the next few years. If the war were to end quickly, much of that security premium would go away, and prices would probably fall to some degree. But they will never go back to where they were before this war boosted them through the roof.

# Society

The consequences of Iraq will not be felt only in our politics and economy. The least predictable arena for postwar America will in many ways be the social one. Every society seems to react to disaster somewhat differently, but the most common ramifications are usually negative. The social fabric of seventeenth-century Spain was heavily damaged by its unsuccessful war in the Netherlands. Although of course it is difficult to make reliable, direct connections between the war and any individual aspect of society, as the military situation in the Low Countries deteriorated, riots broke out in many Spanish cities, scandals wracked the government and military, crime increased, youth became disillusioned, and drug abuse became a widespread problem.[33]

The United States experienced quite similar problems in the 1970s. Vietnam was the defining moment for what has become known in some circles as the "culture wars," which pit the forces of tradition against those of liberalism over issues like gay rights, the corrupting influence of the entertainment industry, and even the meaning of Christmas. The influence of the anti-war movement in the United States in bringing an end to the war cannot be quantified—it is quite possible that the hippies and collegiate protestors repulsed the majority of Americans and actually hurt their own cause—but there is no doubt that their voices gave impetus to the rise of a countermovement, which was most memorably symbolized by the "Moral Majority" of Reverend Jerry Falwell. The *Roe v. Wade* decision, which legalized abortion in every state was viewed by many conservatives as the tipping point, the defining moment of the counterculture era. The religious right became a force in American politics as a direct response to the dangerous free-love, drug-infested, leftist, anti-war movement that emerged in the 1960s. Overall, then, Vietnam created divisions that went far deeper than politics, ones that have lasted for decades. As the longtime *Time* magazine critic Robert Hughes observed, even in the world of art "the nightmare of Vietnam cast America into an age of anxiety from which it has not yet emerged."[34]

The extent to which any society will be affected by defeat is once again inversely related to the strength of that society: While the strongest of countries sometimes hardly feel the effects and rebound quickly, defeat can often shake weak societies to their very foundations. Soviet society proved to be incapable of absorbing the seemingly inconsequential defeat in Afghanistan. Levels of alcoholism and depression, which were already high, surged while public confidence in government fell, and the Communist Party itself followed soon thereafter. When stressed, the Soviet Union imploded, with a speed that was terrifying to those with any knowledge of Russian history. Great powers usually do not go gentle into that dark night, and political change in Russia had usually been exceptionally violent. But go gentle it did. Afghanistan, more than any other single factor, provided the impetus for Gorbachev to reform his system, which of course led to the collapse of the USSR and the end of the Cold War. "The decision to leave Afghanistan was the first and most difficult step," recalled the last Soviet foreign minister, Eduard Shevardnadze. "Everything else flowed from that."[35] The Soviet Union proved to be a fragile, brittle country, one that was unable to cope with major shocks.

Relative levels of casualties seem to have little impact upon the extent of social disruption. The Soviet Union lost somewhere between thirteen and fourteen thousand soldiers over the course of nearly nine years in Afghanistan, which was less than it lost on many individual days during World War II. More French people were killed driving on roads while the war in Algeria raged than were killed by Algerians.[36] More Americans were killed on D-Day than are likely to die in Iraq. But the knowledge that casualty rates are small by historical standards appears to be small comfort to societies that have experienced a military disaster. Any deaths in a losing cause are too many to bear. Defeat's effects always go far beyond rational calculation.

Iraq is thus likely to cause a certain degree of social turmoil in the United States. Over time, the so-called culture war divide will probably grow worse. The conservative and liberal forces in American society are quite unlikely to reach any major reconciliation in the aftermath of this disastrous war. Indeed, they will probably soon grow to distrust one another even more. But overall, the United States in the twenty-first century remains undeniably strong, and is predisposed to be able to recover from disaster more quickly than most countries. Iraq will serve as a test, but it surely will not be one that the United States cannot eventually pass.

## THE PEOPLE AND THE PRESS

To most members of American society, modern warfare has become very much like a spectator sport.[37] The vast majority of us watched the war in Iraq unfold on television, from the safety of our living rooms. Only a little more than one tenth of one percent of our population did any of the fighting, and few have been directly, or even indirectly, affected. Images from the front were so heavily sanitized, at least in our media, that one could have been forgiven for occasionally forgetting that real suffering lay behind the statistics. The role that the media has played in this war has been controversial from the very beginning.

In October 2007, retired General Ricardo Sanchez, who served as commander of Coalition Authority forces in Iraq from June 2003 through June 2004, kicked off what appeared to be a publicity campaign for a forthcoming book by delivering a scathing, semi-coherent rant about the culpability of both the press and the Bush administration for the debacle. Sanchez was of course blameless, despite the fact that he presided over many of the decisions that went so poorly early on in the war and was the commander ultimately responsible for the Abu Ghraib scandal. It was the media, not his leadership, that had created an "environment that does a tremendous disservice to America."[38] How dare they report his blunders.

The media has historically been everybody's punching bag. To those on the left, the "embedded" members of the media were some of the war's biggest cheerleaders in its early stages. To those on the right, the media has been actively working to undermine the Bush administration from the moment it took office. It has been the media's steadfast refusal to report all the "good things" happening in Iraq that has fed a false image of chaos and disaster, according to this view, and that is what has driven the public to despair. As is always the case, when the message is unpleasant, the messenger can expect to receive some of the blame.

The intensity of the naturally competitive relationship between the media and the government has waxed and waned over the years. Vietnam was something of a turning point, at least in the twentieth century, since there was much more cooperation between the two before that war than there was afterward. The press and the government enjoyed a respectful and in many ways mutually beneficial relationship before Vietnam; but as the 1960s wore on, that relationship began to fray and turn more acrimonious. Washington and the Fourth Estate entered Vietnam as partners, but they left it as adversaries.

A new generation of baby boomer journalists certainly contributed to this change. Most of the fault, however, lay with the way the Johnson and Nixon administrations sought to portray progress in the war. Today we would politely call this "spin" or, much less politely, "outright lies." Prominent war correspondents like David Halberstam and Neil Sheehan were quite supportive of the war in its early stages, but soured over time when faced with a gaping chasm between what they were witnessing on the ground and what they were hearing from official U.S. sources. "The White House," Halberstam was to write afterward, "was putting its word against a handful of reporters in Saigon . . . the journalists very quickly came to the conclusion that the top people in the embassy were either fools or liars or both."[39] Soon thereafter, the *New York Times* received and decided to publish what became known as the Pentagon Papers, which of course exposed a line of official thinking on the war that did not match public statements. Since then it has become almost an article of faith in journalistic circles that the government cannot necessarily be trusted to tell the truth during times of war, and in government circles that the press cannot be relied upon to support the nation during crises.

While playing "watchdog" over the government has always been part of the media's job, after Vietnam the importance of that role was raised to new heights. It was this new contentious relationship that helped to bring down the presidency of Richard Nixon. Bob Woodward and Carl Bernstein were products of the post-Vietnam era, and were therefore predisposed to assume that the administration would lie whenever it felt it could get away with doing so. Prior to the war, the press may well have accepted the president's word at face value; afterward, no one was willing to believe much that any administration would say.

Watergate was at its essence a third-rate burglary, an expression of paranoid politics that has no doubt been a fixture in Washington since its beginnings. In the highly charged, divisive political atmosphere created by Vietnam (and fed in no small part by Nixon's actions), public outrage exploded. It is very difficult to imagine how this otherwise rather minor peccadillo could be enlarged to the point where a president would fall, were it not for the stockpile of public anger that already existed because of the war. Had Nixon won the presidency in 1960 and perpetrated this stupidity then, no explosion would have followed and he would have kept his job. In 1973, much of America was still in the throes of the anger stage, and was eager to punish its leaders. Watergate gave the people that opportunity. Although Nixon was to lament the rise of "adversary journalism" after his fall from grace, it was anger generated by Vietnam that created the conditions for its rise.[40] By failing to pull out when he had his chance, Nixon had unwittingly dug his own grave.

For a generation, all American media coverage of war has been interpreted through the prism of Vietnam. The military today seems to regard the press as something of a necessary evil, one that can be friend as well as foe. As a result, the media no longer has unrestricted access to the battlefield, or the freedom to find its own story and determine its own independent truth. Still, the restrictions are far less stringent for the second Gulf War then they were for the first, and there has been no shortage of journalists willing to risk their lives bringing far corners of this war to light. Well over a hundred have been killed in the process. At this stage, the relationship between the media and the government does not seem to be growing worse as Iraq goes on. It went in shaky, and will likely come out the same way.

The presence of an independent Arab media adds a welcome layer to the overall message, one without the rather bizarre American reluctance to show casualties. Critics of the U.S media should recall that the rest of the world does not seem to believe that war can be accurately covered devoid of suffering. American audiences have seen precious few of this war's dead and wounded on their television screens. *The Washington Post* even received a great deal of criticism for showing closed, flag-draped coffins on their way to their final destinations back home. American dead are presented as names, not faces; after attacks, the tally of casualties makes the news, but not images of the blood that was spilled. Iraqi civilian casualties—the hundred thousand who have died by violence and untold thousands whose lives have been cut short by the war's many disruptions—are equally anonymous. An observer may well come away with the impression that there is actually very little pain and suffering going on in Iraq. But not even such heavy media sanitization has proven capable of sustaining public opinion.

The role of the Fourth Estate in contributing to disaster in Iraq has already become the subject of a certain amount of pointless debate, especially between those on the right who accuse it of crimes just short of treason, and those on the left who insist that it merely serves the interests of its corporate masters. As was the case with Vietnam, the media will provide those who bungled the United States into war with a convenient target upon which to deflect blame. And just as with Vietnam, the way the war is covered will actually have very little effect on its ultimate outcome. Blaming the messenger is only necessary when the message is awful, and the messages coming out of Iraq have been pretty awful since the very beginning.

## THOSE DOING THE FIGHTING: RETURNING, STILL SERVING, AND NEVER TO RETURN

What of the brave men and women that America has sent over to Iraq? Surely they will face adjustment challenges of an entirely different magnitude than the rest of the public, most of whom did not have their daily lives altered in any significant way by the war. Corson noted after Vietnam that the return home for those who have been defeated by an inferior foe is especially painful. When beaten by a peer, "soldiers come home disconsolate and cautious about their personal future, but if they have fought well at least their honor is left intact." After an upset, however, soldiers "come home like thieves in the night, social outcasts without even the solace of knowing theirs was an honorable defeat."[41]

The United States seems to be (justifiably) ashamed by the way its Vietnam veterans were treated after the war. After Iraq, the atmosphere is likely to be starkly different. The rabidly anti-military left was quite small throughout this war, and even the most passionately anti-war activists seemed to regard military personnel as victims of this tragedy rather than perpetrators of some sort of capitalist crime. While the mantra "support the troops" was often consciously conflated by hawks with supporting the war, there was little doubt that the United States was prepared to treat its returning soldiers with the honor they deserved. Modern politicians compete to determine who is the most supportive of the men and women in uniform. No officer can testify to Congress without being thanked gratuitously by each member. Even Joe McDonald, the iconic Vietnam-era protest musician from Country Joe and the Fish, has gotten into the act, urging America to "Support the Troops" in his 2005 protest song. The American people were making it abundantly clear that although they no longer supported the war, they certainly appreciated the sacrifice their all-volunteer military has made in waging it.

The proper treatment of veterans was one of the very few universally accepted, rather uncontroversial lessons this country learned from Vietnam. The men and women who will return from the Gulf can expect to be admired and profusely thanked for their service. None of this madness, after all, was their fault. Their adjustment period will likely not be without pain, of course, but one can hope that the support of a grateful nation will help to minimize their suffering. The loss of national honor can hopefully be kept separate from their sense of personal honor. To the extent that it proves impossible to salve their emotional wounds, their pain can be considered another lingering casualty of this ill-advised war.

We also understand a great deal more about post-traumatic stress disorder (PTSD) than we did a generation ago. As a result, the haunting image of the homeless, deeply troubled Vietnam veteran begging for booze money will hopefully not be repeated by Iraq war vets in the years to come. Although there have been complaints about the veterans' support system and exposés on Walter Reed Hospital in *The Washington Post*, the American people could take some solace in the rather undeniable fact that the treatment of returning soldiers will likely be better than at any time in the past, for any nation.

What of those currently serving in Iraq? Does talk of defeat and disaster hurt their morale? Among the troops fighting in Iraq are many of my former students, from both the Naval Academy and the War College. I keep in touch with more than a few, some of whom have asked me what I think they should be telling the men and women they command, given my general views on the wisdom of this war. I have always responded the same way: To be honest, I have no idea. I don't know what advice to give to those leading troops in this war, or what to tell to a nineteen-year-old private seeking meaning in the Iraq madness. But I do know this: There should be little fear of damaging the morale of the U.S. soldier and Marine in Iraq. They are professionals; they will do their job, and do it extraordinarily well, no matter what direction the political winds blow back home. They are part of the best armed force in world history. And they know that this nation is profoundly grateful for their service, whatever the outcome.

Finally, and perhaps most importantly, I also do not believe that a withdrawal from Iraq would mean that our fallen soldiers, among whom are some of those former students, have died in vain. It is simply not true that sacrifice is only meaningful and justified when it is part of a winning cause. If one believes, as I do, that there is honor and nobility in fighting for one's country, then the ultimate outcome of the war is not particularly relevant in evaluating the worth of the sacrifice. Were the United States to pull out of Iraq, the lives lost will not have been lives wasted. "That our effort in Vietnam proved unwise," Robert McNamara wrote of veterans of that war, "does not make their sacrifice less noble."[42]

It would no doubt horrify those who have fallen if their memory were used to put more men and women in harm's way on behalf of a pointless cause. We owe it to those still in the field to bring them home as soon as it becomes clear that our goals are unachievable. In Iraq, that moment has long passed. America cannot let some imagined and ill-advised debt to the dead outweigh the actual responsibility it has for the living.

THE WAR IN IRAQ will continue to poison the politics, economics, and social fabric of the United States as long as there are troops fighting and dying in this lost—and utterly pointless—cause. Iraq is an open wound that will slowly bleed over the course of the next decade and beyond, if we allow ourselves to continue in the same strategic direction. It is now clear to all but the most stubborn that the goals the United States hoped to achieve through its invasion of Iraq are no longer achievable. To continue pressing on without realistic hope is unfair to our taxpayers, allies, and above all to our soldiers, who now fight for a cause that is unattainable at best and profoundly misguided at worst.

None of the outcomes discussed in this chapter is inevitable. In fact, even the most likely of negative consequences can be prevented. The mere awareness of the likelihood of increased partisanship can help us minimize its effects, for instance. Economic pessimism should be tempered by the knowledge that because of globalization, the global financial system is more resilient than ever before. And perhaps if we understand the psychological stages that people go through following a defeat, the social effects will be easier to manage. The United States will survive defeat in Iraq, without question. But the amount of pain it must suffer along the way is largely up to its people, and its leaders, to determine.

# 3

◇

# A Republic, If They Can Keep It

## CONSEQUENCES FOR IRAQ
## AND THE MIDDLE EAST

O N THE FOURTH ANNIVERSARY of the invasion of Iraq, President Bush repeated his oft-expressed belief that the consequences of a premature withdrawal would be "devastating" for American security.[1] Senator John McCain wholeheartedly agreed, although he preferred to use the words "catastrophic," "disastrous," and "grave."[2] Few critics of the war have ever questioned that assessment. Those who argued for an immediate pullout did not doubt catastrophe, but rather just seemed willing to live with the inevitable, dire consequences.

Indeed, if one belief has been able to unite all sides of the various debates about the war, it has been this: Were the United States to remove its troops from Iraq, geopolitical and humanitarian disaster would soon follow. The region would be swept into unprecedented chaos, lawlessness, and internecine violence. Sunnis and Shi'ites would form battle lines and fight a genocidal final battle; al Qaeda, safely out of the reach of justice, would be able to attract recruits by the thousands and go on the offensive; war would spread throughout the region and beyond, arriving eventually at our own shores. Terrorism would increase and oil prices skyrocket, alongside a humanitarian catastrophe of unparalleled intensity. Little wonder, then, that the president "surged" troops into Iraq, redoubling U.S. efforts to bring stability to the region.

Fortunately for a nation on the edge of defeat, none of those catastrophes is particularly likely, even if the United States were to pull its troops out immediately. While the consequences of defeat on the home front may turn out to be more serious than we expect, there are good reasons to believe that the ramifications for international security will be far less serious. And even if some of these worst imaginable, unlikely scenarios do occur, the implications for U.S. security would be minimal. Although we seem to believe that our interests are tightly bound together with those of the Middle East, in reality little that happens over there has direct effect on the way we live our lives over here. It is rather curious that even normally sober analysts have let themselves become convinced about the likelihood of a horrible series of post-withdrawal disasters, none of which is ever subjected to much scrutiny. The final outcome in Iraq will not be pleasant for the region, but it is not likely to be catastrophic, either.

In order for the United States to move past the initial, acrimonious stages of post-Iraq development, it will need to pull its troops out of Iraq and admit that the operation was a disastrous mistake. Continued occupation driven by visions of apocalyptic disaster should not be given the benefit of the doubt.

# A Brief History of the Future

All policy choices are based upon implicit predictions about what is to come. If, for example, like President Bush one believed that the overthrow of Saddam Hussein's regime was likely to produce a healthy, market-oriented democracy—say, a Japan—in five years, a nation that presented a shining example for the region and decreased anti-American hostility in the Arab world, the choice to go to war would have been an easy one to make. If on the other hand one believed that war in Iraq would create an untenable situation, a festering wound of a guerrilla war that would fan the flames of fundamentalism, who in their right mind would have lent support? The president's vision of the post-Saddam future was decisive in the process of making the choices that led to war. Evaluating predictions is therefore one of the most important tasks facing any decision maker.

While no one can say for certain what the future will bring, those who study prediction in international affairs can offer three simple, practical rules that should assist those who carry the awful burden of making foreign policy decisions. None are absolute, of course, but they do help separate likely outcomes from unlikely, and should allow policymakers to calculate realistic policy risks. All three suggest that the outcome in Iraq is likely to be less catastrophic than the pervasive pessimism suggests.

First, and perhaps most obviously, policymakers should keep in mind the rather basic observation that *the unprecedented is also unlikely*. Outliers in international behavior do exist, but in general the past is the best guide to the future. Since the geopolitical events that pessimists expect to follow U.S. withdrawal are all virtually without precedent, common sense should help policy-makers conclude that they are probably also unlikely to occur. Five years ago, U.S. leaders should have realized that their implicit predictions about the aftermath of invasion—positive, creative instability in the Middle East that would set off a string of democratic dominoes—were events without precedent. The policy was based more on the president's unshakable faith in the redemptive power of democracy than on a coherent understanding of international relations. Before the war, realists argued that, like all faith-based policies, success in Iraq would have required a miracle; unfortunately, in international politics miracles are rare events. Faith is once again driving predictions of post-withdrawal Iraq, but this time it is faith in chaos and worst-case scenarios.

A second important observation about the future, and one that is particularly salient for Americans, is that *our imagined consequences are usually worse than what reality delivers.* As we have seen in previous chapters, human beings tend to focus on the most frightening scenarios at the expense of the most likely, and anticipate outcomes far worse than those that actually occur. Prospect theory helps us understand why people focus on the potential negative outcomes of defeat. Since people are motivated more by the desire to avoid losses than to make gains, losing looms larger in our calculations than probability would suggest it should. But the mere fact that the obsession with unlikely negative outcomes is understandable does not mean that it should be allowed to drive U.S. policy choices.

For some reason, U.S. policymakers seem to be especially prone to overestimate the threats they face. Throughout history, the threats perceived by U.S. leaders have almost always been quite out of proportion to actual, tangible dangers lurking in the international system.[3] We have intervened in Central and South America scores of times in large part because, since at least President Monroe's time, we have obsessively feared the spread of European influence in our hemisphere. During the Cold War, overblown fears propelled us to become convinced that the fate of countries like Vietnam, Mozambique, Grenada, Angola, and El Salvador somehow affected the security of the United States. We have elevated one weak, two-bit dictator after another, from Qaddafi to the Ayatollah to Kim Jong Il, to the status of almost Hitlerian evil. More recently, our leaders seemed to feel that the continued existence of a weakened, prostrate Saddam Hussein somehow represented a gathering danger to the most powerful country in the world. Prewar Iraq was thus no exception to this pattern of exaggeration; postwar Iraq is not likely to be, either. Until we separate the likely consequences of withdrawal from the unlikely, we risk becoming hostages to our rather irrational fears yet again.

The third observation about prediction is one that is echoed throughout this book: *The natural human distaste for defeat distorts rational evaluation of likely outcomes.* Policymakers can easily fall into the trap of envisioning war to be a contest of wills rather than politics by other means, to paraphrase Clausewitz's famous dictum, which tends to encourage the pursuit of victory for victory's sake, whether or not the interest of the nation is served. All countries are therefore likely to continue fighting long after the war ceases to serve their interest. This pattern is certainly repeating itself in Iraq. We are not getting out in part because we just don't like to lose.

Three major complex catastrophes would follow failure, according to current conventional wisdom: regional chaos, which might spread the war and empower Iran; humanitarian disaster for the people of Iraq; and increased Islamist terrorism, at home and abroad. We will consider the first two here and the third in the next chapter, all the while keeping the three observations in mind. Fortunately for the people of America and those of Iraq, the consequences of the U.S. defeat are likely to be quite a bit less catastrophic than we have long been led to believe.

## Regional Chaos

It is sometimes said that war is God's way of teaching Americans about the rest of the world. Since 2003, those Americans who have bothered to pay attention have learned lessons about the different ethnic groups that exist in Iraq and across the Middle East. They have learned more about Islam than they ever thought they would, and especially about the division between Shi'ites and Sunnis (which the president himself may have been unaware of until two months before ordering the invasion).[4] They have become familiar with a long list of previously unfamiliar places, like Fallujah, Ramadi, al Anbar, Basra, and Tikrit. And they have learned that left to their own devices, without the calming presence of the United States, the people of the region would immediately turn on one another. The slaughter would be unimaginable.

Without the U.S. presence, so this conventional wisdom goes, nothing would be able to prevent Sunni-vs.-Shi'ite violence from sweeping into every country where the religious divide exists. A

Sunni bloc with centers in Riyadh and Cairo might face a Shia bloc headquartered in Tehran, both of which would face enormous pressure from their own people to fight proxy wars across the region. In addition to intra-Muslim civil war, cross-border warfare could not be ruled out. Jordan might be the first to send troops into Iraq to secure its own border, but it would be far from the last. Once the dam breaks, Iran, Turkey, Syria, and Saudi Arabia might well follow suit. The Middle East has no shortage of rivalries, any one of which might descend into direct conflict by a destabilizing U.S. withdrawal. In worst cases, Iran might emerge as the regional hegemon, able to bully and blackmail its neighbors with its new nuclear arsenal. Saudi Arabia and Egypt would soon demand suitable deterrents of their own, and a nuclear arms race would envelop the region.

Fortunately, none of these outcomes is particularly likely.

WIDER WAR

No matter what the end state in Iraq turns out to be, the region is not likely to devolve into chaos. Although it might seem counterintuitive, by most traditional measures the Middle East is a very stable neighborhood, both internally and externally. Continuous, uninterrupted governance is the norm across the Middle East, not the exception; most of the region's regimes have ruled for decades. Its monarchies, from Morocco to Jordan to every Gulf state, have generally been in power since these countries gained independence. Their staying power has been rather astonishing, as the table below illustrates.

If regime longevity is any indicator of political stability—and it should be—then by far the most politically unstable countries

## YEARS IN POWER FOR MIDDLE EAST LEADERS/FAMILIES, TO THE END OF 2007

| | | | | | | | |
|---|---|---|---|---|---|---|---|
| Saudi Arabia | 76 | Libya | 39 | Qatar | 36 | Iran | 18 |
| Jordan | 52 | Oman | 37 | UAE | 36 | Yemen | 18 |
| Morocco | 52 | Syria | 37 | Egypt | 26 | Algeria | 9 |
| Kuwait | 47 | Bahrain | 36 | Tunisia | 20 | | |

in this region are Israel and Lebanon, which are also the only two democracies. The autocrats of the Middle East have been more likely to die quiet, natural deaths than meet the hangman or post-coup firing squad. Saddam Hussein's reign was unusual in both its duration and how it met its end: It managed to last only twenty-five years, a short tenure for this region, and it was overthrown violently. The other regimes have survived potentially destabilizing shocks before, and they would probably be able to do so again. The widespread impression that this region is full of weak states teetering on the edge of collapse hardly matches reality.

In addition, the region experiences relatively low levels of cross-border warfare, ethnic conflict, and civil war. Since the end of the Cold War, the Middle East has been quite calm, at least by its historical standards. Saddam once again proved to be an exception, as did the Israelis with their misadventure in Lebanon. But it is worth remembering that four wars were fought between Israel and its neighbors in the first twenty-five years of its existence, and none has been fought in the thirty-four years since. Vicious internecine wars that once engulfed Lebanon and Algeria have been relatively quiet. Its level of ethnic conflict hardly makes the region unique—in fact, outside of Iraq there is no such conflict anywhere in the entire Middle East. Overall, the perception that the Middle East is a massive tinderbox waiting for the right spark (like a U.S. defeat in Iraq) to set it alight is simply not accurate.

No state in the region is likely to prove eager to replace the United States as occupier of Iraq. As much as the Saudis and Iranians may threaten to intervene on behalf of their co-religionists, they have never shown much desire to invade and duplicate the American counterinsurgency effort. If the U.S. troops were to leave, both countries might well provide support and training to their allies in Iraq, but they would be quite unlikely to send in their armies, which would surely meet with the same kind of Iraqi nationalism that surprised the neoconservatives (but not, of course, the realists). No matter what happens in Iraq, no other state is going to plunge into the vacuum created by a U.S. withdrawal and spend itself into oblivion in the quixotic attempt to prop up an inevitably unpopular puppet regime. If the United States with its remarkable military and virtually unlimited resources could not bring about its desired solutions in Iraq, why would any other country think it could do so? Why would anyone want to repeat America's terrible mistake?

In reality, no one in the region wants to see an abject implosion in their neighborhood. All of the Middle Eastern rulers share a common (and rather understandable) fear of chaos, which if allowed to fester might eventually feed revolutionary ideas into their otherwise docile people. If the United States were to withdraw its forces, increased regional cooperation is far more likely than outright warfare that might exacerbate the situation further.

Common interest, not the presence of the U.S. military, will provide the ultimate foundation for regional stability.

## TURKEY AND THE KURDS

Prior to the invasion of Iraq, realists warned that the overthrow of Saddam Hussein would do serious damage to Washington's strategic relationship with Ankara, because the Kurds who live in northern Iraq would be very likely to increase their support for the long-standing Kurdish rebellion in eastern Turkey. That conflict, which had been quiet since 1998, would explode anew if the Kurds gained de facto independence. Neoconservatives assured us that no such exacerbation of tensions would occur, since Iraq was going to be a democracy when the war was over, and democracies get along with one another. As it turned out, the overthrow of Saddam Hussein did serious damage to Washington's strategic relationship with Ankara, because the Kurds increased their support for the long-standing Kurdish rebellion in eastern Turkey. Surprise, surprise. At the beginning of 2008, U.S.-Turkish relations stood at a lower point than at any time since World War I.

A U.S. withdrawal need not lead to a Turkish invasion of northern Iraq, however. It is a bit puzzling that anyone would believe that no incentive structure could be devised to convince Turkey not to attack its neighbor. Withdrawal of its troops would after all hardly rob the United States of all the tools with which it can influence regional events. Washington and the rest of NATO still wield a significant amount of influence over Ankara, especially since a cross-border invasion would almost certainly imperil Turkey's prospects of entering the European Union. In addition, the United States could do more to help the situation by pressuring its new allies in northern Iraq to crack down on the operations of the main perpetrator of the increasing violence in Turkey, the Kurdistan Workers' Party (PKK), which has for years been on the State Department's list of foreign terrorist organizations. This situation has put Washington in a bind, since northern Iraq was the lone success story of the invasion, and remains fiercely pro-American. In a region where the United States has few allies, the Kurds have been a welcome exception. Nowhere on earth (including in the United States) has President Bush been more popular since 2003 than in the Kurdish-controlled areas of Iraq. Some influential analysts have even suggested that the United States should redeploy troops to northern Iraq, in order to deter Turkey and reward our new Kurdish allies.[5]

For realists, this suggestion is a rather preposterous nonstarter. The strategic relationship that the United States maintains with Turkey far outweighs any imagined moral obligation to help the Kurds. A U.S. presence in Kurdistan would force the United States to do one of two things: Either try to root out terrorists (or freedom fighters, depending on one's position) from Kurdish society, which would obviously embroil U.S. troops in yet another local, intractable conflict; or allow the continuation of state-sponsored terrorism in a NATO ally. Instead, the United States should resist the temptation to believe that it has an obligation to look out for the fate of the Kurds. After all, the postwar outlook for the Kurdish people is brighter than ever because of the sacrifices made by the United States. Theirs is a debt that they can never fully repay; one step in the right direction, however, would be to crack down on the PKK. Somewhere between thirty and forty thousand people have died in violence between Kurds and Turks since the mid-1980s, and passions are understandably high on both sides. Kurdish grievances about the way they have been treated at the hands of the Turks are no doubt justified, but the use of violence to address them is not. Further support of the United States should be earned, not given without strings as part of a misguided partial withdrawal plan. The obvious fact that the long-term strategic interest of the United States lies more with the Turks than the Kurds ought to be made quite clear to our sometimes underappreciative allies in northern Iraq. The removal of de facto U.S. protection would presumably encourage the Kurds to act more responsibly toward their more powerful neighbors, and may well prove to be good for regional stability.

A full-scale Turkish invasion of the north is far from inevitable. Should such an assault occur, however, it would not have much direct effect on the security of the United States. As much as we all would like to see peace and prosperity everywhere, the passions in that part of the world run at a higher level than Americans can truly understand. The Near East is where ethnic hatred exists in its purest, most deadly form. A Turk-Kurd war would be awful for the innocents caught up in the fighting, and the West ought to bring its non-trivial economic and diplomatic clout to bear in order to prevent it. But in the final analysis, the conflict is not our business. Bringing peace to every corner of the globe, even those whose stability we have wrecked through our own incompetence, is not necessarily in the strategic interest of the United States.

## THE ELEPHANT AND THE MOUSE

One of the great truths in international politics is that small countries and big countries never really understand one another. The weak cannot ever fully trust the strong, since one mistake can lead to the destruction of their country; the strong, on the other hand, can never comprehend the level of paranoia that their overwhelming power creates in the weak. It is only by keeping this in mind that we can understand the dynamics of the relationship between Iran and the United States.

For the hard-liners in Tehran, the war in Iraq has been a godsend. Over and over again, one hears that the real victor of this war will be Iran, and with good reason: Its regional clout has risen, nascent democratic movements have been silenced, and Iranian credibility in the broader Islamic world has received a boost as the United States floundered. But there is little reason to believe that Iran would emerge as the new ruler of the Persian Gulf if the United States were to admit defeat and leave Iraq.

Iranian influence over its neighbor is consistently overstated. While it is true that many of the new Iraqi leaders have strong ties to Iran, and that a majority of Iraqis are Shi'ites, nationalism will keep the two apart. Iran is not an Arab state, after all. Iraqis have little desire to be ruled by Persians, who are nearly as foreign to them as are Americans. Neither Iranians nor Iraqis have forgotten the eight-year, bloody war they fought against each other in the 1980s that took the lives of over a million of their young men. In international politics, my neighbor is typically my enemy (and neighbors of my neighbors are my friends); there will be no mad rush inside Iraq to replace U.S. presence with Persian. Our fears of Iraq becoming an Iranian protectorate are overblown.

Iran foments instability in its neighbor not so much because it is eager to fill a postwar vacuum with its own troops but because it has little interest in seeing an unfriendly, weak Saddam Hussein replaced with an unfriendly, strong democracy. Tehran will seek to keep Iraq divided, just like any state would probably do in its position. It knows that it cannot expect to dictate policy for Baghdad, nor will it be able to bully the other Arab states into following its orders. There is a natural distrust between Iran and the rest of the region, one that will likely prove to be a bulwark against any aggressive Iranian expansion.

It may prove very difficult for the United States to resist the temptation to elevate the backward, medieval Iranian regime into our next enemy *du jour*. Iran may be the main state sponsor of terrorism in today's world, and its government certainly continues to espouse a rather extreme form of Islam, but the case that Iran poses a real threat to the interests of the United States falls apart upon close inspection. Its economy is in shambles, with most sectors centrally controlled and remarkably inefficient. About 90 percent of its population receives its income from the state. Both unemployment and inflation rates are in the double digits.[6] Iranian military spending rose dramatically following the U.S. attack on Iraq, but it still is only around $10 billion per year.[7] The United States, by comparison, spends around $650 billion, once the costs of Iraq and Afghanistan are factored in. The Islamic Republic may be able to stave off collapse for as long as petrodollars keep flowing in, but it will never be able to mount anything resembling a serious challenge to U.S. power. Iran is a weak country that is important only to the extent that we make it so. Wise policy, therefore, would ignore it, which we could begin to do once we got out of Iraq.

Iran has seen its neighbors to the east and west attacked and quickly conquered. It made a series of diplomatic overtures to the Bush administration following 9/11, which were apparently answered with its inclusion on the "axis of evil."[8] Any war between the two would last about a half hour, and both sides know it. Perhaps it is little wonder, then, that Tehran has decided to seek the ultimate equalizer: nuclear weapons.

There has been, and will be in the future, serious pressures from right-wing circles in the United States for military action to prevent the Iranians from developing nuclear weapons. Tehran has supposedly been "six months away" from an atom bomb since I was in junior high. Even the remarkable National Intelligence Estimate of 2007, in which the many members of the U.S. intelligence community stated their consensus view that the Iranians halted their weapons development in the fall of 2003, did not prove to be persuasive enough to convince proliferation pessimists that an Iranian bomb is not right around the corner. Cooler heads might suggest that in the final analysis it may prove impossible to knock Tehran permanently off the road toward nuclear weapons, and that the United States would do better to try to determine how it will deal with, rather than prevent the emergence of, a nuclear Iran. Not only are the military options unlikely to work, they are also profoundly unnecessary.

Realists see no reason to believe that the Iranians would be much different from any other state if they obtained nuclear weapons. The theocrats in Iran have the same top priority as any other ruling group: self-preservation. Never before in the history of the world has any country committed suicide. No leader has ever worked his or her way up the ladder of government to achieve the top position only to kill himself and his countrymen. Gross miscalculation has of course occurred—Saddam Hussein comes to mind—but never intentional national suicide. Nuclear weapons tend to concentrate the mind, virtually eliminating the possibility of miscalculation. Leaders know that if they use these weapons, they will be destroyed in an overwhelming response. Any Iranian use of nuclear weapons would be suicidal, not accidental. And entirely unprecedented.

Were they to acquire a nuclear weapon, the leaders of Iran would not launch it against Israel unless they were prepared to see their rule, and their desire for a Shi'ite power bloc, come to an end. Giving a bomb to Hezbollah or Hamas would be the functional equivalent of using it, because nuclear explosions leave radiation "signatures" that can be traced back to their point of origin. There would be no way to plausibly deny who gave these groups their bombs, and Tehran (or at least the regime) would still face retaliation. *Realpolitik* therefore counsels that even theocrats would act rationally with the ultimate weapon, no matter how much bluster may emerge from bombastic leaders.[9] What Iran *does* is far more important than what its clownish president *says*. And overall, Iran—like every other country—tends to act in accordance with its national interests. Destruction of the state is certainly not one of those interests.

Few serious analysts believe that the Iranians would actually use nuclear weapons, were they to develop them, or even give them away to those who would. The main concern about a nuclear Iran is that it would be able to blackmail its neighbors, or step up regional adventurism, since its weapons would free it from fear of any serious retaliation. But as the Cold War demonstrated, the leverage that nuclear weapons provide is minimal, since interaction and even conflict can occur without either side choosing to "go nuclear." In fact, nuclear weapons are all but unusable in most situations, since they virtually guarantee the destruction of whatever regime decides to employ them.[10] International behavior actually changes little when nuclear weapons are present. In 1973, for example, the Egyptians knew that Israel had nuclear weapons, but they decided to attack anyway, under the assumption that nuclear weapons would not be used. The Gulf States would be safe in calling Iran's nuclear bluffs, should it ever come to that, or responding with force to provocation. And both sides know it. Nuclear weapons would not substantially affect the balance of power, or behavior of countries, in the Gulf.

Would an Iranian bomb lead to runaway regional proliferation? After all, there is a certain amount of prestige that nuclear weapons provide to the state that develops them, which might begin to cause some jealousy in the region. Saudi Arabia and maybe even Iran's other regional rivals might feel that it was in their interest to counter the Persian bomb with an Arab one, setting off a destabilizing regional nuclear arms race. Presumably, however, the United States would be able to affect Saudi calculations, if and when Iran goes nuclear, perhaps through extensions of security guarantees (the so-called nuclear umbrella). Surely the Saudis, who are one of our closest regional allies, can be made to feel safe from Iranian nuclear attack. Proliferation fears are almost always overblown. The nuclear club has remained about the same size now for nearly a generation.[11] Even if it were to prove impossible to dissuade the Saudis from purchasing a bomb (since they show no interest in making one on their own), one should not be convinced that it would mean the end of the world. Deterrence logic would still maintain stability in the Gulf.

But we are getting ahead of ourselves. Iranian nuclear weapons are hardly inevitable. In fact, *if we were truly interested in seeing their program shut down, we would get our troops out of Iraq posthaste.* Our presence in Iraq raises the threat level in Tehran, and makes an Iranian bomb more likely. Defense planners in Iran surely make the reasonable calculation that the only long-term guarantee against someday meeting the same fate as their neighbors is a nuclear deterrent. It is entirely rational that they would want one, and this would be the goal of any Iranian regime, whether it be a democracy or theocracy, as long as the threat posed by the United States seems to be so high.

If the Iranians go nuclear, it will not be because they were emboldened by our defeat. It will be because of the fact that we attacked in the first place, rebuffed their overtures for peace, and kept troops within sight of their border. The Bush administration hoped that making quick work of Saddam Hussein would send messages to other unfriendly capitals across the region, and encourage better behavior; instead, Iranian nukes may well be one more unpleasant outcome of our Persian Gulf blunder.

## PERSIAN GULF OIL

Iraq is in the middle of the most important resource region in the world. Major disruptions in the flow of Persian Gulf oil can obviously have immediate, worldwide economic consequences. Historically, economic performance in the industrialized world has been inversely related to the price of oil: high prices restrict its economies, while low prices tend to promote growth. Therefore, maintaining a healthy flow of oil from that Persian Gulf has always been high on the list of U.S. priorities. Would defeat in

Iraq throw the world oil market, which is already tightly stressed, into chaos?

While short-term disruptions may occur in the wake of a U.S. defeat, the Persian Gulf oil trade is more stable in the long run than is commonly perceived. There is little reason to believe that a U.S. military presence in the region is necessary to assure that its oil gets to anxious consumers. It is in the interests of all parties involved—the producers, the middlemen, and the consumers alike—to keep Persian Gulf oil flowing, no matter what the political situation might be. Oil does no one any good in the ground. Since war can obviously create turmoil in oil markets, and since the Gulf States cannot survive long without the influx of hard currency, any instability that emerges would probably prove to be quickly brought under control. No common interest unites the major oil producers more than the need to assure that the spigot will always be on.

Furthermore, and perhaps counterintuitively, cross-border warfare to control the territory that contains fossil fuels is exceptionally rare. It is surely not impossible, of course, as Saddam's Kuwait misadventure demonstrated, and outright conquest is not the only way that the flow of oil can be disrupted. Sabotage, intimidation, terrorism, and other kinds of economic warfare all could interfere with the oil trade and cause steep fluctuations at the pump. However, instability in the region has not always resulted in disruptions of supply. Even the 1980–88 Iran-Iraq war failed to have much of an impact on oil production, despite the fact that much of the fighting occurred within artillery range of major oil terminals and facilities.[12] In addition, surely a good case can be made that the cost from rare and temporary supply reductions would never outweigh the long-term benefits in savings that pulling the U.S. presence out of that region would bring. Would oil price volatility cost the United States more than $2 billion per week, which is what is currently being spent in Iraq?

Even domination of the Persian Gulf by unfriendly powers, while unlikely, would not prove to be much of a threat to oil production. No matter who is in charge of Saudi Arabia, or Kuwait, or even Iraq, there is every reason to believe that they will always have strong incentives to sell their oil to the industrialized consumer states. In one of the very few studies of this issue, political scientist Shibley Telhami found that "a change in regime from moderate to radical in one state does not appear to alter the pattern of that state's foreign trade."[13] Throughout the Cold War, the nature of Gulf regimes had little or no impact on who they traded with, or how much. In other words, market forces have a greater impact than national policy in determining the flow of oil. Any government determined act with profound economic irrationality would be quickly displaced by domestic rivals eager to maximize profits from oil revenue.

Further, unlike in years past when boycotts could target individual countries, modern oil companies control distribution and will make adjustments to keep their customers satisfied and protect their profits—2008 is not 1973. Today, market forces, not political machinations, determine price and distribution of oil.[14] Unfriendly dominance of the Gulf (which, again, is quite unlikely no matter what happens in Iraq) would not alter the fact that producers of oil must sell in order to benefit. As long as that remains true, the United States will never be cut off from the source of its energy addiction.

In fact, a reduction of the U.S. presence in the Persian Gulf might well have positive long-term ramifications, since it would force the industrialized world to consider reducing its dependence on imported oil. Few events would spur more investment in new exploration and alternative sources of energy, both of which are long overdue, than the prospect of a drawdown of U.S. hegemony in the Gulf. Calls for energy independence based upon quite logical strategic, economic, and environmental reasons have been ubiquitous since 9/11, but little of substance has been accomplished. Nothing is likely to change in the current strategic environment.

Perhaps we could learn a lesson here from Hernando Cortés, the Spanish conquistador who in 1519 burned his ships in order to motivate his men to move forward into the forbidding, frightening Mexican interior. Perhaps the United States needs to take a Cortés approach to oil security, burning its ties to the Gulf in order to force this reluctant nation onto what might be a long road to energy independence. By leaving the Gulf States to fend for themselves, the United States would send a clear signal that there is no turning back from the mission at hand. Sometimes brazen acts are required to concentrate the national mind.

## THE AFTERMATH OF VIETNAM

This is of course not the first time that the United States has worried that military failure would lead to catastrophic geopolitical consequences. Throughout the war in Vietnam, U.S. policymakers consistently warned that defeat would have wide-ranging, serious ramifications for U.S. security. Dominoes would fall into the Communist camp across Southeast Asia and beyond, eventually perhaps even reaching our own shores. Despite these dire warnings, popular pressures eventually forced the United States to withdraw its forces from Southeast Asia and to cut back on its aid to the region. Washington stood by in horrified silence as North Vietnamese troops overran Saigon in 1975. Many analysts warned that this disgraceful "cut-and-run" would bring about a string of foreign policy disasters for the United States. If Vietnam was as important as those on the far right maintained, then the 1970s would likely have seen evidence of allies beginning to question U.S. commitments and increased levels of Soviet activity in the Third World. The conventional wisdom suggests that the humiliating rooftop helicopter evacuation from the U.S. Embassy in Saigon should have heralded the beginning of a dark period for the United States and the free world.

However, the defeat did not lead to the long-predicted spread of communism throughout the region and beyond, as even Kissinger today (perhaps grudgingly) acknowledges.[15] On the contrary, in the ten years that followed the fall of Saigon, the non-Communist nations of Southeast Asia not only avoided falling prey to Communist revolts but enjoyed a period of unprecedented prosperity.[16] The only dominoes that fell were two of Vietnam's neighbors, Cambodia and Laos, both of which were hardly major losses for the West, especially given the tragedies that followed.

Some postwar analysts have argued that a string of negative outcomes did in fact occur in the 1970s as a direct result of the U.S. defeat in Vietnam. Nixon lamented the Communist successes in Laos, Cambodia, and Mozambique in 1975, as well as those in Angola in 1976, Ethiopia in 1977, South Yemen in 1978, and Nicaragua in 1979.[17] Kissinger even suggested that our irresolution encouraged Islamists in Tehran to overthrow the Shah.[18]

It seems that with enough creativity every negative event of the decade, no matter how distant it may have seemed to be, can be connected back to the defeat of our South Vietnamese allies. Such revisionist history, though perhaps an article of faith in hawkish circles, cannot withstand even the shallowest scrutiny.

First of all, it is not at all clear that any of these reversals was at all related to the U.S. defeat in Vietnam. The Communist insurgencies in Cambodia and Laos were raging alongside that in South Vietnam, and are perhaps better thought of as parts of a regional war. Communist success in what was Indochina did not spread to Thailand or Indonesia, much less to India or Japan, as the hawks had feared. As prewar realists anticipated, nationalism provided a firewall that stopped the spread of communism, one which could not be overcome by any post-Vietnam loss of confidence in U.S. commitments.

Presumably Saigon's collapse had little to do with the fall of the Ethiopian monarchy, or the final destruction of the Portuguese Empire in Africa, which was the factor that led to Marxist gains in Mozambique and Angola.[19] Opposition forces, which were predominantly leftist in all three countries, took over in the vacuums of power. No one has ever presented any evidence to support the notion that either South Yemeni or Nicaraguan rebels acted because of post-Vietnam perceptions of the United States. The fall of the Shah to Khomeini's fundamentalists in 1979 is the greatest stretch of the domino theorist's imagination. The connection between Vietnam and Iran must be accepted on faith alone. It is just as plausible—in fact, far more plausible—to believe that these events were unconnected, and that they would have occurred no matter what had happened in Saigon in 1975.

Just as importantly, only the most inveterate Cold War pessimist would consider any of these "gains" to have been substantial advancements of the Soviet cause. The list of additional Communist bloc allies included some of the few countries that were even less relevant to the international balance of power than was South Vietnam. The addition of Angola, Mozambique, South Yemen, and Ethiopia to Moscow's sphere hardly strengthened the Soviet Union's position. If anything, these poor and needy countries served as a drain on Soviet resources, which was clearly not something that its brittle system could easily handle. The countries lost to the free world after Vietnam not only were irrelevant to U.S. security, they actually proved to be beneficial, since they placed strains on the USSR's weak economy.

Finally, it is not at all clear that geopolitical momentum was actually on the Soviet side in the 1970s. Just as prospect theorists would have predicted, contemporary U.S. analysts and historians of the period have tended to focus more upon losses than gains. Consequently, the decline of U.S. influence in Ethiopia has loomed larger than the simultaneous increase in Somalia. Soviet fortunes were also reversed in Egypt, the Central African Republic, and Ghana, but no one took much notice.[20] In fact, there was only one instance of a meaningful shift in the 1970s, and it was in a positive direction for the United States. Nixon's visit to China in 1972 and the subsequent warming of relations were abject disasters for the USSR. Unlike Mozambique, Nicaragua, or Laos, China actually mattered. And while it did not become a close ally of the United States, it is clear that Beijing turned decisively away from the Soviets. Overall, when poor countries shifted toward the West, their movement was considered to be irrelevant by those on the right; when Communists gained power, however, it was evidence of post-Vietnam disaster.

Contrary to widespread concerns at the time, and to the historical revisionism of the hawks, international geopolitical disaster did not follow defeat in Vietnam. Not only did catastrophe fail to accompany the collapse of Saigon, but the Cold War ended in Western victory fourteen years later. The worst fears of those making de-escalation decisions proved to be entirely unfounded. Unprecedented chains of dominoes did not fall, despite our worst-case scenario fears driven by the natural distaste for losing. As it turns out, Vietnam was all but irrelevant to international politics, which is of course exactly what realist critics of the war had maintained all along. Iraq is likely to prove equally inconsequential.

Overall, a regional descent into the whirlwind following a U.S. withdrawal cannot be ruled out; using that logic, neither can a string of benevolent transitions to democracy. Just because a scenario is imaginable does not make it likely. In fact, most of the chaotic outcomes pessimists predict require unprecedented breaks with the past, which makes them rather unlikely to occur. Since the United States has historically overestimated the threats it faces, there is every reason to believe that it is doing so once again. Sagacious policy should always take into account most-likely scenarios, not the worst-case fantasies devised by a nation whose judgment is skewed by the specter of losing the war in Iraq.

## Humanitarian Disaster

The second major catastrophe that people fear would follow a U.S. withdrawal from Iraq is a large-scale humanitarian disaster.

Without the presence of U.S. troops to bring a measure of stability to the region, we are told, the forces of chaos would be set loose, unleashing all manner of anarchy and bloodshed. The security analyst Stephen Biddle argued in *Foreign Affairs* that "genocide is a real possibility" in the wake of a U.S. withdrawal, and that the "risk of mass slaughter is especially high."[21] James Carafano of the Heritage Foundation has warned of "Rwanda writ large."[22] By implication, apparently, Rwanda was writ fairly small—its 800,000 deaths would pale in comparison to the bloodbath that would overwhelm Iraq.

Throughout history, predictions of post-defeat bloodbaths have commonly surfaced to support the argument to continue fighting, especially among those who generally refuse ever to admit failure. Over two hundred years ago, after the decisive battle of Yorktown, hawks in the British Parliament warned of the thousands of Loyalists who would be slaughtered if the redcoats were withdrawn. No such slaughter occurred.[23] Nearly two centuries later, President Nixon warned in November 1969 that a precipitate U.S. withdrawal would be followed by massacres by a victorious North Vietnam. At a press conference six months after that, he said that removing American troops would "allow the enemy to come into Vietnam and massacre the civilians there by the millions, as they would."[24] One often hears echoes of Vietnam in the debate today, in warnings that the United States has a moral obligation to prevent a repeat of the post-1975 slaughter of its South Vietnamese allies. "One unmistakable legacy of Vietnam," President Bush told a veterans group in the summer of 2007, "is that the price of America's withdrawal was paid by millions of innocent citizens whose agonies would add to our vocabulary new terms like 'boat people,' 're-education camps,' and 'killing fields.' "[25] The haunting precedent of post-Vietnam slaughter has been repeatedly used to bolster the arguments of those urging perseverance in Iraq.[26]

However, the vast majority of scholars, journalists, and analysts who have investigated this slaughter—from the far right to the far left, from official U.S. government sources to independent journalists—now agree that it never took place, at least not on the scale that is commonly believed.[27] Ho Chi Minh City was obviously not a pleasant place to live in the decade that followed its name change, and the Hanoi government established a number of "re-education camps" where the suffering was surely substantial. And certainly a percentage of those who fled the country in boats died along the way, perhaps numbering in the tens of thousands. But there was no large-scale, genocidal bloodshed of the kind predicted by pessimists.

The myth of widespread postwar slaughter was born in 1985, when two academics at UC Berkeley claimed that sixty-five thousand Vietnamese civilians were killed between 1975 and 1982.[28] After publishing their findings, both scholars were awarded with posts in the Reagan administration. Their figure has been repeated—and enlarged—by revisionists ever since, despite the fact that it was subsequently proven to be grossly exaggerated, and a product of especially shoddy, partisan "scholarship."[29] The myth of the post-Vietnam bloodbath has nonetheless become an article of faith for the far right, who consider it to be further proof that the only thing standing between innocents and the reaper is Uncle Sam in his white hat. If anything, the chaos, reprisals, and violence that Vietnam experienced in the aftermath of its civil war were somewhat less serious than is the norm following such conflicts, which are usually the most vicious kind of war. Reconstruction in the United States was, after all, hardly non-violent.

It was particularly difficult to follow President Bush's logic when he attempted to connect the Khmer Rouge's genocidal "killing fields" with the U.S. withdrawal from Vietnam. In fact, the Lon Nol government of the early 1970s was one of the very few in the world even more inept and corrupt than that in Saigon. There were few on either side of the political aisle who were suggesting at the time that American troops be transferred from Saigon to Phnom Penh to help stave off its inevitable collapse. Without U.S. involvement in the region, there may not have been a coup that overthrew Prince Sihanouk in 1970 in the first place, and thus no Lon Nol, and no Khmer Rouge.[30] It was the U.S. intervention in Southeast Asia, not its withdrawal, that contributed to the killing fields.

Overall, there is little reason to believe that the rather limited number of American troops is all that stands between the Iraqi people and genocide. The bloodletting in Iraq could be worse than it is under the current U.S. occupation, of course; increased violence not only cannot be ruled out, it is probable in the short term. However, the United States should not operate under the old saw that "the devil we know is better than the devil we don't," since the devil we know currently results in the deaths of many Iraqi civilians every day. Short-term paroxysms of bloodshed can sometimes be preferable to slow, long-term bleeding.

Fortunately, such paroxysms are probably not very likely to begin with. After all, much of the ethnic cleansing in Iraq has already taken place. The violence in Iraq dropped dramatically in the closing months of 2007, largely because the people had either segregated themselves into defensible enclaves or fled. This may have ended forever the neoconservative dream of a functioning, flourishing democracy, but it made stability in Iraq more imaginable. The worst days of the civil war may well be behind us. In the long run, one of two outcomes is likely in the wake of U.S. withdrawal: political accommodation; or a civil war that eventually *someone wins*, which would bring an overdue end to the bloodshed. Neither can happen as long as U.S. troops are present in Iraq, prolonging its agony. Only Iraqis can bring stability to their country, and they cannot begin to do so until we get our troops out of the way. Our departure would actually speed the return of normalcy for the people of Iraq.

The United States would of course reserve the right to return in the unlikely event of an outbreak of Rwanda-like genocidal fury, where innocents were at risk of being slaughtered by the hundreds of thousands. We would always be able to punish the guilty, or merely make their lives quite miserable, without too much trouble. No free hand should ever be given to genocidaires. But such future reintroductions of force probably would never be necessary, in part because the United States will also be able to wield its rather non-trivial economic and diplomatic power, both of which could affect future Iraqi events in important, positive ways. A withdrawal of our troops would hardly spell the end of our influence in the region.

Overall, we will never know if our presence is indeed the only thing preventing humanitarian catastrophe in Iraq unless we pull out and let events take their course. It is equally if not more plausible to believe that stability will once again return only when outside forces stop supporting an unnatural, unsustainable imbalance. Perhaps, then, we should choose the less expensive course.

## OUR RESPONSIBILITY

The United States is obviously not without moral obligations in Iraq. Perhaps most importantly, America should not abandon those Iraqis who worked for democracy in their country, those unfortunate few who believed our promises and supported our effort to spread freedom and combat evil. As the United States fled Vietnam, it unconscionably left thousands of former allies behind to fend for themselves, many of whom languished for years (if they were lucky) in re-education camps. Surely we can learn from these mistakes. Washington has a clear duty to assure that those who wish to leave Iraq are able to receive the visas that will allow them to do so. Thus far, however, the Bush administration has steadfastly resisted allowing Iraqis to resettle in the United States. In March 2007, while the State Department claimed that there were 1,500–2,000 Iraqi refugees "being processed" for admission to the United States, the Council on Foreign Relations reported that *only 500* visas had been granted since the beginning of the war.[31] Sweden has allowed far more Iraqis to enter its country than has the United States.

Why has the United States turned its back on the people it has promised to help, now that it is clear that the help has failed? In part, we have not wanted these people to flee from Iraq and in effect abandon the effort to transform their society. Granting visas to Iraqi refugees would be a sure sign of the failure of the grand neoconservative experiment. By now, however, there is presumably little need to fear one more sign of failure, since there is no shortage of others. A green light for green cards would send the wrong message for an occupying power; once that occupation is called off, such calculations can change.

But it probably will not, at least until new leadership comes to Washington. The Bush administration sent a clear, unmistakable message that it simply did not want Arabs coming into this country. The far right does not typically welcome non-white immigrants, and since 9/11, Muslims have topped the list of undesirables. Any Iraqi exile community in the United States would apparently be considered too much of a security threat during our "war on terror." President Bush in effect told the world that he cares deeply about the fate of Iraqis . . . as long as they stay over there, where they belong. Even those who risked their lives and their families translating for American troops have been told to seek refuge elsewhere.

The American people should not let their government abandon and betray our Iraqi allies. We have thoroughly broken what was an already weak Iraqi society; the very least we can do, on our way out the door, is take along those whose only mistake was becoming convinced by the Bush administration's promises of freedom. Surely there is room in our country, and in our hearts, for those we have betrayed.

## ON POWER AND LEVERAGE

Most of the interested local actors, from Shi'ite tribal leaders to Iraqi parliamentarians to Saudi monarchs, have always had strong incentives to exaggerate the likelihood of post-withdrawal chaos. It is in fact in their interest to have Washington believe that civil war, regional chaos, and genocide would inevitably occur without U.S. troops, which prevents their removal. No one in the region has any real incentive to improve the economic, political, or security situation in Iraq, therefore, since this might well convince Uncle Sam to leave and take his money and his security forces with him. Unless they want to assume responsibility for the region's future, Iraqi leaders need to scare Americans into staying with visions of chaos.

Our unconditional commitment unintentionally, but entirely predictably, set up a perverse incentive structure that has encouraged the Iraqi government to stall and backslide. From the outset of the war, the Bush administration assured the Iraqis and the rest of the region that U.S. forces will not leave *until* stability arrives. Instead, what the administration should have been telling local actors is that its forces will leave *unless* stability arrives, which would have provided a clear incentive for the various factions to make real progress.[32] If we had reserved the right to leave from the outset, we could have long ago provided incentives for cooperation in the parliament, competence in local security forces, and aid from regional states and other interested actors.

By pledging to stay engaged in Iraq no matter what the cost and no matter how long it takes, President Bush in effect surrendered what is always a vitally useful tool at the negotiating table: the power to walk away. In any bargaining situation, the ability and the willingness to leave helps shape the choices made by the other side. They will always be more willing to compromise if they know that we might walk away at any time. Instead, Washington basically ceded control of its actions to the locals, allowing Gulliver to be held hostage by the Lilliputians. The United States sacrificed both the flexibility that its overwhelming power ought to have provided and its ability to get weak local actors to do what it wanted them to do. Basic strategic logic would have suggested that the United

States ought to have made the Iraqis earn our friendship and support; unfortunately, such basic strategic thinking was almost entirely absent in the cloistered upper reaches of the Bush administration.

It is never too late to alter the incentive structure facing the various actors in Iraq, all of whom presumably have a lot more to lose from chaos and civil war than we do. If the United States were to make a credible threat to leave, Iraqi minds would be forced to concentrate on solving their problems. Deadlines should be announced immediately, and preliminary preparations made to withdraw. Instead, according to General Petraeus, with the surge the United States is preparing for another decade of benchmark-free occupation. No one should be surprised, then, if real progress in Iraq continues to remain elusive.

WHEN IT COMES TO contemplating the international ramifications of the Iraq disaster, for some reason we often allow worst-case scenarios to receive the benefit of the doubt. As was the case with Vietnam, defeat is not going to be easy for Americans to accept, but it also should not be allowed to fuel our most paranoid fantasies of catastrophe. Life will go on, much like before, for Americans and Iraqis alike. The world will not end; neither will the era of American preeminence.

While no one—least of all any president—likes to lose a war, a good debate on the way ahead cannot take place until the most likely consequences of defeat are separated from the fantastic and the illusory. It is vitally important for policymakers to understand that significant strategic risk would not accompany defeat in, and withdrawal from, Iraq. The unprecedented is also unlikely, and regionwide wars, collapsing Middle Eastern regimes, and expanding terrorism are all unprecedented events, no matter what happens in Iraq. If historical patterns are any indication of future events, Americans are probably overestimating the danger posed by defeat. Those overestimations are prolonging the war's agony, for both the Iraqis and the Americans.

To the degree that the fear of catastrophe following withdrawal from Iraq is related to the human fear of the unknown, it is understandable; to the degree that it is motivated by concern for the Iraqi people, it is noble. Indeed, we ought to have no illusions about what would be most likely to follow a U.S. withdrawal: Continued ethnic cleansing in Iraq until the various sides are able to come to an agreement; increased short-term regional tension; and uncertainty and bitter domestic discord in the United States for a generation. Although the implications of the Iraq war on the home front are likely to be powerful and long-lasting, the American people can take some comfort in the knowledge that the most likely consequences for national security are not nearly as ominous. Strategic catastrophe, and damage to tangible U.S. interests, are simply not likely outcomes, and should not provide the basis for policymaking. The United States must not let fantasies of unprecedented regional disaster drive its decisions about how best to recover from this ill-considered and mismanaged war. One catastrophic error need not beget another.

If we are to move on toward national acceptance of this disaster, we must let Iraq fend for itself. Iraqis must take control of their own fate. They have been given their republic; it remains to be seen whether they can keep it. In the end, it will not be our decision to make.

# 4

---✧---

# Iraq and the "Long War"

M IDWAY THROUGH his second term, in May 2007, President
Bush gave a commencement address/pep talk on Iraq at
the U.S. Coast Guard Academy. Between that speech and the
press conference that followed the next day, he used the words
"al Qaeda" sixty-seven times. Among those words that the president failed to mention were "civil war," "insurgency," "militia,"
"guerrilla," "death squads," "Sunni," "Shi'ite," and "Kurd."
Although Maliki, Sadr, and all other Iraqis whose names are not
"Hussein" were not brought up, Osama bin Laden earned fourteen appearances.[1]

Later that year, General David Petraeus gave his update
on the surge strategy in Iraq to the Senate Foreign Relations
Committee—on September 11, 2007. Perhaps the timing was
merely a coincidence. Perhaps it was merely fortuitous for the
Bush administration that the media covered his testimony amid
the moving tributes to those who had died at al Qaeda's hand

six years before. After all, statistically speaking, there was just as much chance of his testifying on September 11 as any other day.

Perhaps, however, the timing was not coincidental. A cynic might just suggest that the Bush administration intentionally chose that day to report on the war's progress, in order to cement in the public mind one of its central strategic claims, that Iraq is the central front of the "war on terror." The administration certainly wanted the American people to believe that a precipitous withdrawal would boost the global extremist movement in both symbolic and practical ways. The specter of a super-empowered al Qaeda emerging from the ashes of Iraq has been the Bush administration's most powerful argument for staying the course. It is surely the most commonly cited justification for continued occupation.

Is Iraq really a battlefield in the larger war on terror? Would defeat embolden our *jihadi* enemies, encourage them to increase their terrorist activities against the United States, and set back our efforts in the struggle against fundamentalist terrorism? Presumably, there are two reasons why terrorism could rise in the wake of the Iraq disaster. First, perhaps al Qaeda or other unsavory characters could find a convenient "safe haven" in a chaotic, post-withdrawal Iraq. Once they did not have to fear for their safety, they could plot new attacks in other countries and overseas. To use what is becoming a common phrase, we would be letting al Qaeda go "on the offensive," rather than keeping them on the defensive, where they presumably are less dangerous. The enemy would soon follow us home, and terrorism would increase in the short term.

In addition, there may be a long-term danger: Perhaps the symbolic importance of Iraq would embolden Islamist groups to launch new attacks against the United States and its allies. The loss of credibility that would come from an upset defeat would inspire a new generation of fighters to throw in their lot with al Qaeda, just as the Russian defeat in Afghanistan inspired the current wave of fundamentalism. If indeed Iraq is a battleground in World War III, as both President Bush and Osama bin Laden profess to believe, then defeat could prove to be a setback for the forces of good in their struggle against evil.[2]

Luckily, however, levels of terrorism are not likely to rise after Iraq. Our efforts in what has become known in military circles as the "long war" on terror, which is a rather poor way to think about grand strategy to begin with, would not be harmed in any significant way if the United States were to pull out of Iraq.

## Terrorists Gone Wild: "Afghanistan on Steroids"

Perhaps the most powerful argument for staying in Iraq is that a U.S. pullout would lead to state failure and the establishment of a safe haven for terrorist operations across the region and around the world. Afterward, violence would eventually "follow the U.S. troops home." A loss in Iraq would therefore bring the "war on terror" to the United States, and we would be forced to fight them "over here." President Bush has expressed this belief, with minor variations, dozens of times, and it is a common refrain in hawkish circles.

Such fears are probably misplaced, for at least three good reasons. First of all, failed states are rare in world politics. Governance is the rule, not the exception. Second, Iraqis have shown no interest in seeing their country become a new home for fundamentalist extremism. Even the Sunnis have turned against the al Qaeda elements in their midst. Finally, and contrary to popular belief, safe havens do not offer significant advantages to terrorists. In the unlikely event that Iraq were to devolve into a large swath of virtually ungoverned territory, it would not significantly threaten the security of the United States.

## FAILED STATES

Today, we are told, the United States is threatened not by the strength of its adversaries but by their weakness. Those states that cannot control their borders, or that are too weak to act against non-state actors operating on their territory, seem to be of primary concern to Washington. The 2002 *National Security Strategy of the United States* made the case on page one: "America is now threatened less by conquering states," it says (rather awkwardly), "than we are by failing ones."[3] A U.S. pullout from Iraq might leave behind a lawless, ungovernable, anarchic void, where Islamist activity could thrive. This could be thought of as the "Taliban fear," since it is based largely upon what was supposedly learned in the chaotic, post-Soviet Afghanistan, where the Taliban government was too weak to resist the temptations of al Qaeda's money. The *New York Times* columnist Thomas Friedman has repeatedly warned that a pullout would turn Iraq into an "Afghanistan on steroids."[4]

Such reasoning is generally baffling to those who have not forgotten the lessons of *realpolitik*. Realists believe that power, not the lack thereof, is the primary tool with which states can threaten their neighbors. It is bizarre to suggest that failed states present a greater threat to our interests today than successful ones, that we are more endangered by Somalia, say, than by China. Threat is directly related to power; terrorists, though they can cause a great deal of suffering, cannot threaten countries with extinction in the same way that a powerful neighbor can. Weak countries are simply less worrisome than strong.

But even if one is convinced that state weakness really is a threat to the United States, it is important to realize that Iraq is not likely to devolve into complete chaos. Failed states are, after all, relatively rare in international politics. The few examples we have are memorable precisely because they provide the exceptions, not the rule. A post-occupation Iraq might be splintered and all-but-officially partitioned, but it is not likely to turn into a Somalia on the Tigris. Power vacuums in Arab societies tend to be filled especially quickly. Temporary chaos in Iraq following a U.S. pullout may be likely, but Afghanistan-like long-term state failure is not. A government will soon emerge—perhaps three—to bring stability to the country, possibly in the wake of civil war. The new government(s) might resemble Iraqi precedents more than Washington would like, but by that time all will likely have come to realize that stability and effective governance is in everyone's interest. The stability will be welcome, and overdue.

Finally, it is perhaps worth reminding ourselves that the United States displaced a strong central government when it decided to invade Iraq. If state weakness were really our primary concern, then we should have let Saddam stay where he was. After all, there was no fundamentalist element running amok in Iraq prior to the invasion. Al Qaeda in Iraq, as well as this misplaced, myopic concern about state failure, are entirely our own creation.

## AL QAEDA-STAN

Iraq does not seem to be fertile soil for the weeds of radicalism. As bad as the sectarian violence has been, the Iraqi people—Kurd, Shi'a, and Sunni alike—have shown no eagerness to replace Ba'athist tyranny with fundamentalist Islam. Few in the region seem to harbor any illusions about how an al Qaeda–like regime would rule. In poll after poll, Iraqis have expressed no desire to follow an Iranian model of theocratic totalitarianism.[5] Bin Laden may arouse sympathy across the Arab world due to his opposition to the United States, but Iraqis have not demonstrated any wish to have him as their leader. Rising anti-Americanism on the "Arab street" simply does not necessarily translate into sympathy for al Qaeda. Iraq is not like Pashtunistan, the region of western Afghanistan that provides the base and fighters for the Taliban. Its people have always been less conservative, more progressive, and generally hostile to fundamentalism.

The much publicized post-surge events in Anbar Province provide further evidence of al Qaeda's unpopularity in Iraq. Throughout the so-called Sunni Triangle, which had been the hotbed of al Qaeda activity in the first few years of the war, local tribes turned against the fundamentalist, often foreign elements in their midst. Al Qaeda in Iraq appeared to be crippled, if perhaps only temporarily, by the healthy majority of Iraqis who were uninterested in its conservative brand of Islam.[6] If its message and vision of society is not welcome among the Sunnis, one wonders where precisely it will be able to flourish. Shi'ite elements will always be hostile to Osama, whose minions have killed thousands and destroyed some of their holiest sites. Were

U.S. troops to be withdrawn, continuing nationwide purges of al Qaeda seem to be more likely than some sort of broad fundamentalist takeover.

The absolute nightmare scenario for Iraq is a descent into the kind of chaos that engulfed Algeria in the 1990s, where tens of thousands died during a particularly vicious civil war. This outcome is not particularly likely, but it cannot be completely ruled out. Even that, however, would not necessarily lead to a rise in the power of al Qaeda. It is important to remember what Algeria was not, even during its time of high crisis: Despite the presence of fundamentalist elements, it never became a safe haven for the exportation of terrorism. There were a few deadly attacks in Paris in the 1990s, but the Islamists in Algeria as a whole never seemed eager to start a *jihad* against the West. Worldwide levels of terrorism did not grow, despite what appeared to be a convenient safe haven for extremists.

The Bush administration's case for staying the course in Iraq rested on a pair of seemingly contradictory claims: First, since the surge convinced the Sunni tribes to turn against al Qaeda, Iraq has turned the corner, and the United States and its allies are winning the war against extremism. However, if the troops were to leave Iraq, the country would be turned over to Osama bin Laden. Defeat would, in the president's words, "surrender the future of Iraq to al Qaeda."[7] The American people allowed the adminstration to have it both ways: We accepted that the surge was successful in defeating al Qaeda in Iraq, but also that Osama would have taken over immediately upon our departure. Overall, the latter claim was more difficult to justify.

## THE MYTH OF SAFE HAVENS

In the post-9/11 era, it became popular in security circles to compare modern Islamic fundamentalist terrorism with piracy. Analogies were commonly drawn between al Qaeda and the Barbary pirates, the group that harassed shipping in the Mediterranean two hundred years ago until the Jefferson administration sent the Marines to the shores of Tripoli.[8] The lesson was always this: Pirates were only able to operate because they had a state sponsor, or at least a state that was willing to tolerate their existence. Al Qaeda was only able to exist, the analogy suggested, because the Taliban allowed it to operate freely in Afghanistan. Generally speaking, when terrorists have a safe haven, their attacks become more likely. Safe havens supposedly allow terrorists space from which to plan offensive actions, rather than concentrating on defense. They can use such safe space to train, assemble weaponry, direct operations, recruit, and eventually launch attacks. Preventing Iraq from offering such a haven, therefore, ought to be at the top of the priority list for the United States.

However, there is good reason to doubt that safe havens are necessary for the perpetration of terrorism, or even that they make attacks more likely to occur. For one thing, the training that a terrorist needs is obviously rather minimal compared to that of a regular army. Basic instruction on explosives is often the only necessary skill, and it is one that does not require a safe haven, as Palestinian groups amply demonstrate. A garage appears to be sufficient. Those skills displayed prominently on al Qaeda propaganda videos, which feature recruits swinging from monkey bars and crawling under ropes for some reason, are of little utility in the kinds of attacks commonly perpetrated by modern terrorists, most of whom seem to have been able to function quite effectively without much training at all. No safe haven was necessary to perpetrate the 9/11 attacks, for instance. The cells that planned and perpetrated the hijackings could have presumably done so whether or not Osama was safe in Kandahar. Sanctuary for terrorists was apparently not necessary to execute the multitude of attacks that have occurred since the deposition of the Taliban, from Madrid to Bali to London, nor is a safe haven a sine qua non for the daily attacks in Iraq. In fact, the vast majority of terrorist groups throughout history, from the IRA to the Basque ETA to the anarchists a century ago, have been able to operate in hostile territory, without any havens in which to swing on monkey bars.

Apparently, being on the "defensive" is not a catastrophic impediment to the would-be terrorist. The connection between safe havens and the ability to perpetrate acts of terrorism abroad is vastly overstated in the current strategic conventional wisdom. Therefore, we would have little to fear if indeed lawlessness and anarchy swept over Iraq, at least as far as terrorism is concerned.

## FOLLOWING U.S. TROOPS HOME

"We left Vietnam, it was over; we just had to heal the wounds of war," argued Senator John McCain on behalf of the conventional wisdom. "We leave this place [Iraq] . . . and they'll follow us home. So there's a great deal more at stake here in this conflict in my view. A lot more."[9] If the senator is correct and the violence in Iraq would follow U.S. troops home, then no rational policymaker would ever end the war before the violence subsided.

Fortunately, he is wrong. So wrong in fact that were it not for his unimpeachable reputation for being a serious strategic thinker, it would be easy to dismiss his statements as merely empty-headed campaign rhetoric. Still, Senator McCain and the others who make this claim must know that terrorists will not follow our troops home in any meaningful way. Intelligence assessments should not be required to cast serious doubt upon the idea that a post-withdrawal United States would soon have to "fight them over here." Such assessments do exist, of course, but all one should really need is a bit of common sense.[10] The ability of any group to perpetrate acts of terror is a combination of two things: intent and capability. In this case, it is not clear that postwar Iraqis would have either one.

As realists have been trying to explain to this administration from the beginning, it is *nationalism* that propels the vast majority of Iraqis in the resistance movement to struggle with such ferocity, not some mythical existential struggle against the West. Were the United States to leave, so too would the inspiration for their war. Just as Vietnamese nationalists were able to declare victory (and an end to the war) once the Americans left, most Iraqis would stop fighting once the foreign invader was expelled. Presumably they would feel no need to try to conquer America afterward, or to liberate New Jersey from George Bush. Surely it is worth noting that there have been very few incidents of terrorism perpetrated by Iraqis outside their borders, either before or after this war began.[11] Why should we think that will change when we leave?

Foreigners fighting in Iraq might feel somewhat differently. Many of the *mujahedeen* who have flowed into Iraq to fight for Islam have already been purged by locals, but those who survive may indeed have the desire to spread the war to new battlefields once the one in Iraq falls silent. But even if they do have the intent, they will not have the capability to do so. It is immeasurably easier for the average militant in Iraq to attack U.S. forces over there than over here. Acquiring visas to travel to the United States is likely going to prove to be difficult for Jordanians fighting in Iraq, or for members of the Mahdi Army, for that matter.

The idea that terrorism will visit U.S. shores after Iraq is yet another example of politics interfering with strategic discussions. The far right has an obvious political interest in convincing the American people that they will be in great danger if U.S. forces are withdrawn, in order to make sure that they continue supporting the lost cause. Never mind the fact that such suggestions are completely preposterous; if people feel that defeat in Iraq would even have a slim chance of raising our terrorism warnings from orange to red, then they will vote the proper way. America needs to stay on the offensive, we are told. The suggestion that the United States would soon have to fight terrorists "over here" is simply an example of meaningless political theater, one that should be unworthy of serious rebuttal. Politics, as usual, has been the enemy of strategy.

Overall, therefore, even if the most unlikely of worst-case scenarios unfolds and Iraq descends into utter lawlessness, the increase in the terrorist threat to the United States would be minimal. Terrorists are only marginally more effective (and perhaps not even that) when given a safe haven thousands of miles away than they are when operating clandestinely inside a hostile environment. Those who fear the development of a terrorist sanctuary in a post-occupation Iraq must explain why a minor increase in their operational capability justifies a major expenditure of our blood and treasure.

So perhaps a good case can be made that defeat in Iraq will not lead to an increase of terrorism in the short run. But what about the longer term? What of the symbolic meaning of Iraq? Many neoconservatives maintain that the United States and its allies are in the opening stages of a third (or even fourth) world war, one for which Iraq is just an opening battle. Could defeat lead to the destruction of U.S. credibility, embolden our enemies, and raise the risk for terrorism in the future? Might defeat in Iraq eventually lead to other battles closer to home? A brief discussion of the importance of credibility and the "war on terrorism" might be useful in dispelling such fears.

## Iraq and World War IV

During the Cold War, people on both the far right and the far left, who tend to interpret all information through a good-vs.-evil prism, often considered international events to be connected in a giant, interdependent web. To those on the left, the forces of world capitalism were conspiring together in order to maintain the flow of profits at the expense of the masses. Those on the right thought the United States was engaged in a moral crusade against the monolithic Communist movement, headquartered in Moscow, which directed and controlled instability and revolutions around the world. There were no coincidences; to people on both extremes, events all tended to be part of a larger struggle. International politics had a unifying narrative, one which pitted the forces of good against the agents of darkness.[12] Realists of course have always doubted the existence of such linkages, and argued that international events can often be quite independent. Nationalism tends to inhibit the growth of monolithic movements.

The war in Vietnam illustrated the differences between these outlooks quite clearly. To those on the left, the Vietnamese resistance was a heroic effort to repel the forces of global domination; to those on the right, it was merely a pawn of the larger Communist movement, centrally controlled in Moscow. To the realist, the Vietnamese were motivated primarily by nationalism, and were merely resisting an invader. The idea of a monolithic Communist bloc seemed particularly hard to defend as the 1970s wore on, and wars broke out that pitted Vietnam against its equally (if not more) Communist neighbors. The Vietnamese fiercely resisted a Chinese assault in 1979, which was hardly the stuff of which worldwide monolithic movements are made. With the hindsight of history, realism certainly seems to explain the dynamics of the war in Vietnam better than the arguments of those on the far left and right.

It is one of the unfortunate features of international politics, and perhaps of human nature itself, that few ever admit that they were wrong. The right is still as convinced as ever that communism was a monolithic evil, and its disciples now tell us that a new worldwide, interconnected force is emerging to threaten all that is pure and good. That single enemy is, of course, "Islamofascism," which poses a threat of an even greater magnitude than the Communists. Norman Podhoretz, one of the most senior and influential neoconservative thinkers, believes we are in the beginning stages of the *fourth* world war (the third was the Cold War), and that this one is going to be the hardest to win.[13] Former Speaker of the House Newt Gingrich, who is a historian by training, prefers to refer to the current world war as only the third, and feels that the problems America faces today are "fully as great as those that faced Lincoln and Douglas in the 1850s."[14] The former professor has identified a number of different battlegrounds for this war, including India, North Korea, Canada, Miami, Israel, Iran, Estonia (where Russians perpetrated a dastardly cyber attack), and anywhere else evil has raised its head. In Gingrich's mind, events in these areas and many others are apparently connected somehow, which has convinced him that "the forces of freedom are on retreat" and that "the forces that are anti-freedom, pro-dictatorship, and, in some cases, purely evil are on offense."[15] Part of the reason to fear defeat in Iraq, therefore, is to avoid emboldening the forces of darkness.

The conflation of Iraq with the "war on terror" is understandable, and even predictable. When faced with the specter of defeat looming on the horizon, throughout history those who have supported the continuation of unwinnable, unpopular wars have often broadened their appeal by trying to connect them to greater, vital struggles. As part of the attempt to rally the nation behind last-minute, desperate measures, hawks often find it useful to remind the public of whatever the bogeyman *du jour* may be. For example, seventeenth-century hawks warned the Spanish crown of the dangers of losing not only a war to the Dutch, but to Protestantism; a century later, hawks in England worried about the rise of republicanism that would result from a loss of the American colonies; communism was the main threat in Vietnam, not the Vietnamese themselves; and today, of course, we are not so much threatened by Iraqis as by Islamic fundamentalism.[16]

Defeat would therefore be a blow not just to the national interest, but to humanity itself, and to the forces of good.

To a realist, this is the worst kind of pseudo-intellectual hogwash. There are many reasons why Islamic fundamentalist terrorists should not be compared to Fascists or Communists, but the most important one is the difference in power and capability of the movements. "Islamo-fascism" is an absurd term. More important, the events that the Speaker likes to talk about are not only unconnected, they are also typical of security challenges at any given time in history. There is nothing particularly dangerous about our current era, as we will discuss in the next chapter in more detail. Defeat in Iraq will not embolden our existential enemies, or set back the U.S. effort in World War III or IV. In fact, a post-Iraq loss of credibility would not spell much trouble for U.S. or international security at all. In order to understand why this is the case, a brief discussion of what scholars refer to as the "credibility imperative" is in order.

## The Credibility Imperative

Were the United States to withdraw prematurely from Iraq, warned Donald Rumsfeld in August 2006, the consequences for global stability would be catastrophic. Dominoes would fall across the region, and then beyond. "The enemy would tell us to leave Afghanistan and then withdraw from the Middle East," he told the Senate Armed Services Committee. Then "they'd order us and all those who don't share their militant ideology to leave what they call the occupied Muslim lands from Spain to the Philippines."

The harm to the credibility of the United States would be nearly irreparable, and before long the American people would be forced "to make a stand nearer home."[17]

Much of the rationale for continuing the war in Iraq is based upon the belief that, in Rumsfeld's words, "weakness is provocative."[18] According to this line of reasoning, Osama bin Laden and his allies were emboldened by the belief that the United States was a feckless, cowardly "paper tiger." When attacked, effete Americans sue—they send lawyers, not soldiers. The September 11 attacks may even have been prevented, so this logic goes, if President Clinton had responded to earlier al Qaeda provocations with a more determined show of force. Future attacks are only preventable by a determined, consistent, reliable United States that stays on the offensive. Failure in Iraq would demonstrate the opposite, and lead to a steep increase in terrorism around the world.

Former Secretary of State Henry Kissinger has warned that a premature pullout would be "disastrous" for "America's position in the world," and the respite from military efforts would be brief before even greater crises descended upon us.[19] Failure in Iraq would cost the United States "the ability to shape events, either within Iraq, on the anti-*jihadist* battlefield or in the world at large."[20] Kissinger is hardly alone in this belief. The editor of the conservative *National Review* warned that "the consequences of that defeat would be remarkably similar to those in the wake of Vietnam. The prestige of the U.S. government would sink around the world, emboldening our enemies and creating a period of American doubt and retreat."[21] Former Secretary of Defense Melvin Laird has even warned that "the stakes could not be higher for the continued existence of our own democracy."[22]

Newt Gingrich has once again been the most apocalyptic of all: "This is a matter of life and death for the United States."[23]

Why would anyone, much less some of the most experienced observers of foreign policy, believe that a loss in Iraq would cripple the U.S. ability to shape events, or lead to the downfall of our democracy, or even the "death" of America? The answer lies in the continuing importance that policymakers place on the credibility of the United States.

Great powers tend to be insecure by nature. They are always quite conscious of the position they hold in the international system, and spend much of their time and energy seeking to maintain their status. Losing prestige is as unacceptable as losing land or treasure, partly due to loss aversion and partly because the perception of their power affects their ability to wield it. They guard their image, therefore, at least as tightly as they do their gold and their land. Since few events harm an image more than defeat at the hands of a minor power, strong countries are apt to fight on long past the time when the end is clear. Minor wars can take on a life-or-death significance for great powers, even if their material importance is otherwise quite small, because of the implications for the national credibility. As the primary historian of the Dutch revolt explained, "'Reputation,' or prestige, was recognized to have a tangible influence in politics and diplomacy, and Spain feared that acknowledgement of weakness in the Netherlands would decrease her stature as a world power."[24] The Netherlands didn't matter; Spanish credibility, however, did.

Experienced practitioners of foreign policy take for granted the notion that actions taken today can affect (and perhaps prevent) the crises of tomorrow. The messages sent by foreign policy actions can sometimes seem to be more important than the actions themselves, since other states—including current and potential enemies—are watching our every move, making judgments about the credibility of U.S. threats and promises. It is in the vital interest of the United States, therefore, to have its threats and promises remain credible. This belief, memorably labeled the "credibility imperative" by the historian Robert McMahon, is quite widespread and well established in the foreign policy community.[25] According to its logic, defeat in Iraq would deal a catastrophic blow to U.S. credibility, which is the glue that holds the international system together.

This conventional wisdom became the object of a great deal of criticism after Vietnam, however, after the credibility imperative drove the United States to disaster. The Soviet Union was evidently not sufficiently emboldened by the U.S. defeat and loss of credibility to increase its "adventurism" in the Third World. Levels of Soviet involvement in the affairs of other countries showed little appreciable difference in the seventies, when U.S. credibility was low, compared to the fifties and sixties, when it was presumably much higher.[26] In an important study, political scientist Ted Hopf examined over five hundred articles and three hundred leadership speeches made by Soviet policymakers throughout the 1970s, and found that their public pronouncements did not show evidence of a belief that U.S. setbacks in the Third World signaled a lack of resolution. "The most dominant inference Soviet leaders made after Vietnam," concluded Hopf, "was not about falling regional dominoes or bandwagoning American allies, but about the prospects of détente with the United States and Western Europe."[27] Soviet behavior did not change, despite the perception of irresolution

164

that many Americans feared would inspire increased belligerence. Relative levels of credibility made little difference.

Overall, it is rather difficult to identify a time when healthy credibility helped the United States achieve its policy goals or low credibility emboldened its enemies. According to most security analysts who have studied this issue, credibility is largely an illusion, and its actual value greatly exaggerated.[28] *We* have a tough time controlling how *they* perceive us, no matter how comforting it may be to think otherwise. As was the case with Vietnam, Americans should not be concerned about the blow to the national credibility that will be inflicted by the loss in Iraq. If levels of fundamentalist terrorism do in fact rise in coming years, it will have nothing to do with whatever events unfold between the Tigris and the Euphrates.

## THE CREDIBILITY IMPERATIVE IN PRACTICE

The credibility imperative is one of the most powerful, if perhaps misunderstood, influences on U.S. foreign policy behavior. Indeed, it is impossible to understand the rationale behind the uses of American military force since the collapse of the USSR, from the Balkans to the Caribbean to the Middle East, without first recognizing the importance that policymakers still put on the credibility of their threats and promises. The advent of the "long war" on terror has changed nothing; in fact, if their public pronouncements can be believed, September 11 and the war in Iraq have actually increased the amount of attention policymakers pay to national (and personal) reputations. As the American-led Coalition tries to extricate itself from Iraq over the course of the next few years, claims about our credibility and reputation will no doubt take center stage. It is important, therefore, to understand just how concerns for credibility shape, and distort, policymaking. Overall, the credibility imperative affects our thinking in three important, predictable, and profoundly negative ways.[29]

First, *the credibility imperative is almost always employed to bolster the most hawkish position in a foreign policy debate.* Cries of appeasement and of the need to maintain credibility arise almost every time the use of force is proposed in the United States. Critics warned that U.S. credibility would be irreparably harmed if Washington failed to get involved in Vietnam, and then if it did not stay until the war was won; if it did not use air strikes against the Soviet missiles in Cuba; if it did not respond to Bosnian Serb provocations with sufficient force; if it failed to attack the leaders of the military coup in Haiti in 1994; and, of course, if it does not "stay the course" today in Iraq. At other times, hawks have employed the credibility imperative to urge two presidents to use military force to prevent nuclear proliferation in North Korea and to punish the recalcitrant Saddam Hussein.[30] The reputation of the United States is always endangered by inaction, not by action, no matter how peripheral the proposed war might appear to be to tangible national interests. To hawks, the reputation for sound policy judgment never seems to be as important as the reputation for belligerence.

The second observation on the use of the credibility imperative in policy debates is perhaps related to the first: *The imperative often produces astonishing hyperbole, even in otherwise sober analysts.* If the United States were to lose credibility, we are always told, a variety of catastrophes would follow; the falling dominoes would eventually not only threaten vital interests and make larger war necessary but could even lead to the end of the republic itself. The credibility imperative warns that momentum toward disaster can begin with the smallest demonstration of irresolution. In the words of political scientist Dale Copeland, "it is easier to stop a snowball before it begins to roll downhill than to intervene only after it has started to gain momentum."[31] Therefore, even tiny missteps can lead to large-scale disaster.

The examples from even very recent history are legion; indeed, this tendency toward hyperbole seems to be almost irresistible. Although in the 1950s tiny Quemoy and Matsu might have seemed like irrelevant, uninhabitable rocky atolls, if they fell to the Chinese without action from the United States, the resulting loss of credibility would have enabled the Communists "to begin their objective of driving us out of the western Pacific, right back to Hawaii and even to the United States," according to Secretary of State John Foster Dulles.[32] Ten years later his successor, Dean Rusk, wrote that if U.S. commitments became discredited because of a defeat in Vietnam, "the communist world would draw conclusions that would lead to our ruin and almost certainly to a catastrophic war."[33] President Reagan told Congress that if the United States failed in Central America, "our credibility would collapse, our alliances would crumble, and the safety of our homeland would be put at jeopardy."[34] The fall of Vietnam, thought Nixon, "would spark violence wherever our commitments help maintain the peace—in the Middle East, in Berlin, eventually even in the Western Hemisphere."[35] Healthy U.S. credibility is apparently the only thing standing between the world and complete chaos.

Audiences often seem distressingly willing to accept such

statements at face value. Rarely are policymakers or analysts asked to justify these visions, or pressed to examine the logic connecting the present decisions to such catastrophic future consequences. Once policymakers accept the imperative to remain credible, logic and reason can quickly become casualties of fear.

The third and final observation is that *there is a loose inverse relationship between the rhetorical employment of the credibility imperative and the presence of vital, more tangible national interests.* Roosevelt did not feel the need to make reference to the reputation of the United States when he asked Congress for a declaration of war against Japan in 1941, for example. Similarly, Churchill's stirring speeches rallying his countrymen at the darkest hours of World War II did not mention the importance of maintaining the credibility of the realm. When a clear national interest is at stake, policymakers have no need to defend (or sell) their actions with reference to the national reputation or credibility. Simply put, the more tangible the national interest, the smaller the role that intangible factors will play in either decisions or justifications for policy. The credibility imperative drove the United States to use force to assure that Korea, Lebanon, Vietnam, Grenada, El Salvador, and Nicaragua stayed in the camp of free nations despite the fact that none had any measurable impact upon the global balance of power. "El Salvador doesn't really matter," one of Ronald Reagan's foreign policy advisers admitted in 1981, but "we have to establish credibility because we are in very serious trouble."[36] When credibility is the primary justification for action, the interest is usually not vital to the United States.

In sum, when the credibility imperative drives policy, countries fearful of hyperbolic future consequences are likely to follow hawkish recommendations in order to pursue relatively unimportant goals. Policymakers and the public alike are thus wise to beware of the credibility imperative while discussing foreign policy options, question the assumptions it contains, and remain skeptical of the catastrophes of which it warns. We all must recognize that the imperative is typically employed when no tangible national interest exists, and is used as a rhetorical smoke screen to win over otherwise peaceful masses. These lessons apply just as much to the Cold War as to the "existential struggle" that has come afterward.

## THE CREDIBILITY IMPERATIVE AND
## THE WAR ON TERROR

The Bush administration took the credibility imperative to new heights. Clearly, the president believed that his personal reputation was a very important factor in achieving U.S. goals during the war on terror. It is true, after all, that the leadership of al Qaeda has repeatedly cited a lack of resolution in Washington as inspiration for its actions.[37] Bin Laden has accused America of being a nation of cowards that will back away at the slightest use of force. "We have seen in the last decade," he has argued, "the decline of the American government and the weakness of the American soldier who is ready to wage Cold Wars and unprepared to fight long wars. This was proven in Beirut when the Marines fled after two explosions. It also proves they can run in less than 24 hours, and this was also repeated in Somalia."[38] Al Qaeda propaganda tells a version of events in Mogadishu that makes the battle seem to have been a glorious victory by the forces of Islam, instead of a rather one-sided affair that pitted hordes of untrained

Somalis against elite troops of the world's best military. Somalia and Lebanon seem to have become integral to bin Laden's narrative misinterpretation of history. If decreased U.S. credibility has altered the calculations of militant fundamentalist groups, then indeed states combating terrorism would be justified in worrying about the messages that their actions send, and should consider the likely impact that current decisions will have on future crises. Would a pullout from Iraq supply Osama and other radicals with an important propaganda coup?

There are good reasons to believe that the answer is no. First of all, relative levels of U.S. credibility do not seem to have affected terrorist calculations in the past. Islamists have struck when our credibility was presumably high, such as after the successful first Gulf War, the strikes in Kosovo, and the overthrow of the Taliban in Afghanistan; and when it has seemed low, like after Beirut and Somalia. Al Qaeda hardly seems to need demonstrations of U.S. fecklessness in order to be inspired to act. Indeed, it is quite a stretch to believe that if U.S. troops had not been pulled out of Lebanon or Somalia, al Qaeda would have acted any differently throughout the 1990s. If the group would have attacked no matter when the United States pulled out of Somalia—and it is certainly plausible to think that it would have—then perceptions of U.S. credibility are not particularly relevant to predicting its actions. Islamists are not awaiting a great victory before they can be "emboldened" to strike again. If such organizations had the capability to strike, presumably they would do so, posthaste, irrespective of the level of credibility of their great enemy.

Second, al Qaeda's perceptions and descriptions of U.S.

credibility are likely to remain largely unaffected by Washington's attempt to control them anyway. In cases of extreme power asymmetry, such as the situation when terrorist groups face the United States, the strategy of the weak actor must always be based on the premise that although it may not be able to employ tangible assets to win the war, intangible, moral elements will instead prove decisive. For example, since they lacked the military power to force a retreat, the *mujahedeen* in Afghanistan needed to preach that the Soviet Union would prove irresolute in order to convince their fighters that resistance was not utterly pointless. Similarly, bin Laden must paint the United States as a "paper tiger" or no one will rally to his cause. Therefore, no matter what the behavior of the strong actually is, the weak are likely to accuse it of irresolution. Since *jihadi* groups have no hope of success without a certain degree of superpower vacillation, it is unlikely that any amount of credibility will cause these groups to abandon that belief (or hope).

Would a U.S. withdrawal help bin Laden prove the point that he will inevitably try to make about U.S. irresolution? Probably not, since al Qaeda and its allies have never shown much interest in the accuracy of their statements. No matter what the United States and its allies do, bin Laden is likely to twist the truth and argue that each succeeding action is further proof of his claims. Many regions of the world have populations quite sympathetic to the argument that despite its apparent strength, the United States is actually a weak, feminized, immoral, corrupt nation. The Middle East, where conspiracy theories often find wide audiences, is seemingly fertile ground for bin Laden's interpretation of U.S. irresolution. In other words, U.S. actions are not likely to have direct bearing on the interpretation of U.S. credibility in the region, or on the outcome of the war on terror, for better or for worse.

Finally, a loss of U.S. credibility is unlikely to provide a boost for al Qaeda recruiting. The Islamist movement is, after all, hardly devoid of potential rallying cries. Ending the war in Iraq may actually prove to be damaging to terrorist recruiting, since the U.S. occupation appears to be providing inspiration for potential *jihadis* all across the region. Continued unconditional support for Israel provides better recruiting slogans than any withdrawal ever could. Those who believe that extremist recruiting will improve when the United States leaves Iraq should be asked to explain why a pullout would be more useful for al Qaeda than the continuing presence of American troops occupying Arab lands. If Washington is truly concerned about controlling the numbers of Islamist terrorists, the best move is immediate withdrawal.

## CREDIBILITY AND WITHDRAWAL

The Nixon administration made it clear that extrication from the Vietnam quagmire would proceed if and only if it could be done without damage to the national honor. The South Vietnamese had to be capable of defending themselves before a pullout would be acceptable to Washington. Were the United States to withdraw its troops from Vietnam amidst defeat, it would suffer serious harm to its credibility, and global calamity would likely follow. Kissinger had long held that the United States could not pull its troops out without threatening "the political stability of Europe and Japan and the future evolution of the developing countries of Latin America, Africa, and Asia," which depended on the perception of a United States "able to defend its interests and those of its friends. If the war in Vietnam eroded our willingness to back the security of free peoples with our military strength, untold millions would be in jeopardy."[39] The credibility imperative, as usual, counseled continued belligerence and warned of apocalyptic consequences that would follow a failure to do so. As the previous chapter showed, however, the South Vietnamese house of cards collapsed soon after the American withdrawal, and although few policymakers seemed to notice at the time, the anticipated string of catastrophes failed to materialize.

Today, the United States once again finds itself faced with decisions about how and when to withdraw from an ill-advised, increasingly unpopular, and probably unwinnable war. The credibility imperative has predictably been playing a key role in the formulation of decisions regarding the endgame in Iraq. Intangible factors like credibility, reputation, and honor will likely prove to be just as important as the more tangible implications for U.S. security. Fears about the messages that a pullout would send to future enemies will encourage hawkish, uncompromising behavior, and threaten hyperbolic potential consequences for failure.

Overall, even if Iraq were to cause some countries to begin to doubt U.S. credibility, it is hard to believe that fundamentalism would sweep across the region, or that our allies would become so disheartened that they would rethink their allegiance to the United States. During the Cold War, theoretically, states had the option to "flip sides" and rely on the Soviets if they began to doubt the credibility of the United States (few ever did so, of course, and none of any geopolitical importance). Today, it is impossible to imagine that any state would flip sides in the war on terror. If anything, the perception that they could not rely on the United States would likely make other states intensify their effort to fight their local, anti-regime fundamentalists. If states of the region do begin to doubt the credibility of U.S. commitments, which is of course by no means inevitable, Islamic fundamentalist victories are not likely. And while it is obviously preposterous to suggest that the United States would soon have "to fight them at home," or that the continued existence of democracy is at stake, such statements are predictable products of the credibility imperative. Both logic and history suggest that the wise policymaker will disregard the worst-case, hyperbolic, belligerent advice from those under its spell. When credibility takes center stage in the discussion, rationality quickly recedes into the background.

THE UNITED STATES responded to the challenges of global communism and Islamic fundamentalism in many similar ways, despite obvious (if sometimes underappreciated) differences in scale of the threats involved. In both cases, fears of domestic infiltration by fifth columnists may cause domestic overreactions that restrict basic civil liberties. A Manichean, us-vs.-them, with-us-or-against-us mentality has once again overtaken the White House. If it is not careful, Washington could again find itself supporting a variety of unsavory regimes in the name of its global competition as this "long war" unfolds. Perhaps most important, *ideas* lie at the center of both the Cold War and the war on terror, making the "hearts and minds" of neutral parties as important as tangible national security interests. The reputation and credibility of the combatants today seem to be as central to policymakers as they were during the Cold War. As a consequence, the war on terror may also inspire ill-conceived, debilitating wars in the periphery in misguided attempts to control the perceptions of others. History never repeats itself, as Mark Twain may or may not have said, but at times it does rhyme.

Defeat in Iraq will not be a setback in a broader war against evil. Terrorism will not rise, either in the short term or in the long term. Continuing the fight, therefore, would not be done to protect our country, but only our sense of national honor. During the American Revolution, Lord Chesterfield warned of the "terrible encumbrance" of dignity and honor, of "putting false value on these and mistaking them for self-interest; of sacrificing the possible for the principle, when the principle represents a right you know you cannot exert."[40] Today, the United States ignores this warning at its peril.

# 5

---◇---

# The Ghost of Iraqs Yet to Come

## A GRAND STRATEGY FOR
## THE TWENTY-FIRST CENTURY

*You may not be interested in strategy, but strategy is interested in you.*

—LEON TROTSKY

E VERYONE AGREES that many mistakes have been made in Iraq. Neoconservatives and the other ardent supporters of the war maintain that unseating Saddam was the correct choice, but the operation was sabotaged by an incompetent administration, feckless generals, rotten intelligence, and/or deceitful Iraqis. In other words, the invasion was *strategically* sound, but *operationally* flawed. The key decisions regarding troop levels, de-Ba'athification, disbanding the Iraqi army, and the like doomed what otherwise would have been a glorious war.

Fortunately, the American people seem to understand, and historians will certainly agree, that the invasion itself was the primary mistake. It was a deeply flawed grand strategy, not mistaken implementation, that has brought the United States to where it is today. Although fingers of blame will be pointed in all directions in hastily written memoirs, in the final analysis the only choice that mattered was the one to go to war in the first place. There is little reason to believe that better decisions regarding minutiae could have molded the deeply broken Iraqi society into a coherent, democratic whole. The Bush administration was operating according to an international political illusion, one that should be further discredited with every car or suicide bomber that explodes in a crowded marketplace, and every doctor who flees with his family from Baghdad.

While blaming the various operational-level decisions will ultimately prove be a failed rearguard intellectual action, it will nonetheless serve an important rhetorical purpose. Deflecting public ire from the strategy that got the United States into Iraq will allow neoconservatives and their allies to avoid introspection, and fend off scrutiny of their deeply flawed foreign policy vision. It will give their side the ammunition with which to defend themselves in the rancorous times ahead. Just as Vietnam has its apologists, so will Iraq.

Iraq was the result of bad grand strategy; the most basic adjustment of the postwar era should be to put the United States on a better, more sustainable strategic path. The first step toward putting this mess behind us is to jettison the grand strategy that got us into it. A reassessment of the role that the United States should play in the world would not only prevent future Iraqs but would help this country as it moves through the post-disaster stages toward recovery. Indeed, if our grand strategy does not change, and if neoconservatism is still influential in years to come, then Iraq might prove to have been merely round one in the American cowboy's struggle against evil. One thing seems certain: Were our founding fathers here, they would look upon Iraq with horror and judge that the nation they created had fundamentally lost its way. Their advice from long ago can help this nation as it struggles to move forward after Iraq.

## Grand Strategy and the United States

The highest level of strategic thinking, the level at which the decisions about when and where to go to war are made, is referred to as *grand strategy*. Essentially, grand strategies are guides to policymaking. They help leaders identify goals, threats, and options, and aid in decisions large and small. A good grand strategy lays out the basic methods that should be employed in pursuit of national interests, the most important of which are generally security and prosperity.[1] In other words, it defines and prioritizes national ends, and prescribes the means—military, economic, diplomatic, even cultural and scientific—that should be used to achieve them. The operational level of strategy governs how wars are fought; grand strategy determines why, where, and when. There are few more important tasks for any president than setting the nation on the right course, and identifying the proper grand strategy to get it there.

The Bush administration made its policy choices according to a very active, internationalist grand strategy that is sometimes referred to as *primacy*. It is the grand strategy of the neoconservatives, the group of advisers that absorbed a great deal of the criticism thrown the administration's way since the war began. There is a great deal written about neocons, very little of which is strictly accurate.[2] Indeed, today the group has been more defined by its critics than by its members. Essentially the neoconservative grand strategy suggests that one of the primary ends or goals for the United States should be the creation and maintenance of a "liberal world order" based upon democracy, free markets, and the rule of law. They are believers in what academics call hegemonic stability theory, which suggests that international peace is possible only if one country is strong enough to make and maintain the rules. It is up to the United States, in the neoconservative mind, to play the role of a hegemon and deliver the common good of stability and security to an otherwise restless world. The war in Iraq made perfect sense in this context—it was aimed at both punishing a recalcitrant member of the international system and bringing democracy and freedom to the Persian Gulf. The term "neoconservative," therefore, is a significant misnomer. These strategists are quite liberal, believing in the redemptive, pacifying power of democracy, and having faith in the ability of the United States to transform the world into a better place.

Few people object to these ends. Where many part company with the neoconservatives and primacy is in the means they espouse to pursue them, which typically includes a strong forward military presence, and a willingness to act unilaterally when necessary. Their critics also are quick to point out that neocons typically inhabit the far end of the threat perception spectrum, and believe that the dangers lurking in the world are far more dire and pressing than do most other national security analysts. And as previous chapters have shown, like all moralists, neoconservatives also tend to see the world as a struggle between the forces of good (led, of course, by the United States) and those of darkness.

Neoconservatives are hardly the bloodthirsty imperialists that their critics often portray them to be. Were it not for Iraq, most Americans would never have even heard of them. But the disaster has raised their profile to what must be a rather uncomfortable level, drawing scrutiny and a rather harsh backlash. None of this is surprising to those who are familiar with the more traditional grand strategy of this country. One of the primary errors of the neoconservatives was to misunderstand the strategic culture of the United States, which has always been much more restrained, cooperative, and less evangelical when it came to our values. From the very beginning of the republic, the strategic thinking in this country has rebelled against the kind of muscular international activism that brought us into Iraq.

Grand strategy was in fact one of the very few subjects on which the founding fathers spoke with basically one voice. Virtually without exception, these men felt that the United States ought not squander the blessings of geography, and consistently counseled the new nation to restrain itself. The United States could afford to remain aloof from most of what happens in the world, they felt, without harming its interests. The wisest course was to have as little connection with the Old World as possible. The United States was made more or less safe by the oceans; therefore, it should concentrate on its own problems, and be that "shining city on the hill" for all other nations to emulate.

George Washington was perhaps the most adamant about this, arguing in 1796 in his Farewell Address that "nothing is more essential than that permanent, inveterate antipathies against particular nations and passionate attachments for others should be excluded." His "great rule" of strategy was that the United States ought to extend its commercial relations with foreign nations, but have with them "as little *political* connection as possible." All of his contemporaries, even those who were longstanding rivals on almost everything else, echoed this sentiment.

Alexander Hamilton advised Washington that "America's predisposition against involvement in Old World affairs" ought to be a "general principle of policy." Thomas Jefferson was "for free commerce with all nations, political connection with none, and little or no diplomatic establishment." In his 1776 pamphlet *Common Sense*, Thomas Paine wrote that although "Europe is our market for trade, we ought to form no partial connection with any part of it. It is the true interest of America to steer clear of European contentions," while John Adams argued that "we should separate ourselves, as far as possible and for as long as possible, from all European politics and wars." A generation later his son, John Quincy Adams, the architect of the Monroe Doctrine, issued a famous warning to go not abroad "in search of monsters to destroy."

Restraint dominated the grand strategy of this country for its first one hundred and fifty years. The United States was never strictly isolationist, as a number of recent books have reminded us, but it usually resisted the temptation to become involved in political affairs overseas, especially in Europe.[3] During that time, the nation experienced steady economic growth and was unmolested by outside forces, eventually rising to become the strongest of the world's great powers. Strategic restraint served the young nation quite well.

After World War II, a series of decisions were made to alter this traditional strategic approach, and the United States has followed an activist, internationalist path ever since. Each postwar administration has eschewed the advice of the founders, and by the beginning of the twenty-first century internationalism had become imbedded in the national strategic conventional wisdom.

The need for such activism is rarely even examined, much less seriously challenged.

Prior to World War II, U.S. leaders had the viable option of keeping their distance from many of the crises that affected the rest of the world. Restraint was a respectable choice, a proud and responsible strategic alternative to internationalism, not a bogeyman used primarily to paint political opponents as know-nothings and flat-earthers. Within one generation, it went from being the default option of American foreign policy to becoming a pejorative term in grand strategy conversations, a straw man to be readily dismissed rather than an option to be considered. No one wants to be labeled with the "i word." Today, isolationism is more commonly thought of as an era in U.S. history, like Reconstruction or the Depression, rather than as a viable grand strategy.

We should welcome and encourage a return to a grand strategy based not upon isolationism but upon restraint in the aftermath of Iraq. No serious strategist advocates isolation or a complete cutoff from other countries, which was a path that Japan tried to follow from the mid-seventeenth to the mid-nineteenth centuries. The Tokugawa emperors tried to ban all interaction with the rest of the world, including diplomacy, trade, and travel, and their country stagnated and weakened. Strategic restraint is a great deal more serious and complex than isolationism, and far more attractive than usually presented by scaremongering politicians of both right and left. As crisply described by the late political scientist Eric Nordlinger, it would mean a "minimally effortful national strategy in the security realm; moderately activist policies to advance our liberal ideas among and within states; and a fully activist economic diplomacy on behalf of free trade."[4] In other words, strategic restraint would not herald Buchananesque economic protectionism, or an abnegation of our moral responsibilities abroad. Instead, a restrained United States would move forward with two assumptions: That the globalized international economy can function quite well without a U.S. military presence; and that international humanitarian burdens should be shared. This grand strategy would cut back on our military commitments, but maintain strong economic and diplomatic engagement with the rest of the world. It is explained in more detail below.

To listen to some, this would be the worst imaginable outcome of the war in Iraq. Restraint is usually treated like a malignancy that has occasional recurrences rather than a coherent grand strategy. When restraint threatened to break out in times past, it created visions of abject disaster for both the United States and the world. "Millions of people are going to starve to death," worried William Corson after Vietnam, sensing a turn inward. "And Walter Cronkite will tell us that's the way it is. Famine will become commonplace."[5] As it turns out, of course, no such disasters occurred, although Vietnam certainly did make the United States reluctant to intervene in peripheral Cold War conflicts. While hardly isolationist, America in the 1970s was more restrained than it had been at any time since World War II. Potential Cold War challenges in geopolitically marginal places like Angola, Cambodia, Mozambique, and Laos (fortunately) went all but uncontested by the United States. From a strategic perspective, not much came of these far-flung battles. The United States discovered that it could afford to stay out of most civil wars in the Third World without much risk to its interests. Restraint certainly didn't hurt, and final victory in the Cold War was not far off.

After Iraq, America is likely to be similarly restrained in its foreign policy. Pundits and analysts of various stripes will warn against the rise of the dreaded specter of restraint as if it guaranteed instability, war, famines, Hitlers, and genocides. The implications of strategic restraint are far from ominous, however, and it should be welcomed as long overdue. America can cut its military spending and cease providing security for the rest of the world, while still remaining quite active economically and diplomatically. A restrained United States would hardly stop trading with the rest of the globalized world, nor would it abandon its moral and legal obligations abroad. It would merely define threats, interests, and obligations far more narrowly and much more logically, ensuring that catastrophic mistakes like Iraq would never happen again. If the United States wishes to avoid another Iraq, it must come home. Internationalists know—and fear—that when explained devoid of caricature, strategic restraint is extremely popular with the American people. They see its logic and appeal immediately. It courses in their veins, as surely as freedom itself.

## Strategic Restraint

The reality of strategic restraint is far more complex and attractive than the straw man version presented by internationalists. A grand strategy based upon strategic restraint would shape foreign policy decisions along three dimensions. First, and most obviously, restraint would mean *a drastic reduction of U.S. military and political commitments abroad.* It would reject the notion that the United States has obligations to use its considerable power to maintain stability or to spread its ideals where they may not bc welcome. Military spending in particular would be brought into line with current threats to the vital national interests of the United States, which are far less dire than internationalists maintain. Our military could be one third its current size and still be the best in the world by far, and more than able to protect this country from its enemies.

Second, *a restrained United States would play its part—but only a part—in international humanitarian affairs.* Today, the United States is the only country capable of providing significant post-disaster assistance, or transportation for UN forces, or funding for regional peacekeepers. The rest of the world rides freely on the back of the U.S. taxpayer, much to the detriment of our economy. Restraint would not imply disregard for international obligations, only the insistence that such obligations be shared. It would not necessarily demand a withdrawal from international institutions—to the contrary, because such institutions facilitate cooperation and burden sharing, they would be very useful to a restrained United States. America ought not to play the role of unilateral global problem solver, or policeman. The Europeans and the Japanese are presumably as opposed to genocide as we are, but are rarely asked to help prevent it.

Third, strategic restraint *does not imply economic isolation*, or some sort of complete withdrawal from the rapidly globalizing world. In principle, many isolationists have been agnostic about economic policy. Protectionists in the Pat Buchanan/Ralph Nader vein are suspicious of trade and argue that U.S. national interests are best served when its corporations and/or its labor force are protected from foreign competition. Strategic restraint begins with a different assumption: The United States as a whole benefits from trade and open markets, so both should be pursued with vigor. Neither, however, is in need of robust political or military engagement to operate effectively. Rather than economic isolation, restraint recommends "free commerce with all," to borrow Jefferson's phrase, and economic engagement around the world. Free commerce is in the interests of all modern nations and is threatened by none. Today, international trade need not be policed by the armed men from the public sector.

A grand strategy of strategic restraint would rest upon four fundamental strategic assumptions: First, that the United States is basically a safe country, perhaps the safest the world has ever known; second, that international intervention often creates more problems than it solves; third, that military force is often not useful in the pursuit of national interests; and finally, that the actual and opportunity costs of international activism far outweigh the benefits.

## ASSUMPTION #1: AMERICA IS SAFE

Generally speaking, there is a direct correlation between the level of danger perceived in the international environment and support for activist grand strategies. In other words, the more threat a person perceives, the more he or she feels that the United States has to be involved in political affairs abroad. It is no coincidence that those with the highest perceptions of threat to the United States— the neoconservatives—also espouse the most muscular, activist grand strategy. Neoconservatism is born out of a desire to control events abroad, or at least influence them, in order to decrease the threats posed by a variety of enemies. Its most vocal proponents are also those who think that the world is a significantly more dangerous place than it was during the Cold War. The Committee on the Present Danger, a collection of neoconservative überhawks at the vanguard of the attempt to sustain the fear of communism in the 1950s and 1970s, has returned since 9/11 to assure America that it cannot relax, for evil has not gone away.[6] It sees its role as that of a modern-day Paul Revere, to remind us all that the Islamo-fascists are coming, the Islamo-fascists are coming. The American people are apparently always in danger of forgetting about the danger they are in. Their restrained, peaceful instincts have to be battled back at all times.

If the United States really were in great danger, a grand strategy based upon primacy may well be logical and desirable. On the other hand, most strategists would probably agree that in an environment of minimal threats, restraint would make the most strategic sense. The real dispute, then, is over the level of threat that the United States and the free world faces in what strategists refer to as "the security environment."

It seems possible to make a very good case that here at the beginning of the twenty-first century, the level of threat the United States faces in the international system is the lowest in its history. The most basic security problem for any country—invasion and conquest—is certainly not a concern of the United States. In fact, it has been many years since Americans had to worry about an attack from abroad. By 1838, Lincoln was already sagely assuring his countrymen that "all the armies of Europe, Asia and Africa combined, with all the treasure of the earth (our own excepted) in their military chest; with a Bonaparte for a commander, could not by force, take a drink from the Ohio, or make a track on the Blue Ridge, in a trial of a thousand years."[7]

It deserves to be remembered that throughout most of human history, the obliteration of political entities was a distinct possibility. Polities as diverse as Central Asian empires, Greek poleis, and German "princely states" all were at risk of conquest or absorption by powerful neighbors. This is simply no longer the case. Since World War II, precisely *one* independent country has been forcibly removed from the map: South Vietnam, which was barely a country to begin with, in 1975. Today, states seem safe from complete annihilation. The stronger countries are even safer; the strongest is the safest.

But it is not conquest that worries Americans today. A variety of other threats, from terrorism and rogue states to proliferation and drugs, can still emerge from the dark corners of the globe, and all seem to demand our continued international engagement. However, any good realist (or anyone with even a minimal knowledge of history) might observe that the threats of the early twenty-first century are quite absurdly minor when compared to those of eras that came before, and certainly do not threaten the existence of the republic. Obviously no grand strategy would ever recommend a de facto surrender to al Qaeda, or downplay the danger that the group poses to the United States. But a restrained United States would interpret its threat, and that from most of the dangers of today, for what it is: *an intelligence and law enforcement challenge of the first order*, not an existential strategic threat. Terrorists may be able to cause tremendous localized damage and kill thousands of people, but they cannot destroy the United States, much less fundamentally change it. Only the United States itself can do that, through overreaction to the threats posed by terrorists. No matter what happens during the "war on terror," we will not be speaking Arabic when it ends. In fact, the United States faces no "existential" threats, no matter what is sometimes said by those on the far right. America simply does not need to play an active role in world affairs in order to address its basic security, since that security is already all but assured.

One can be fairly confident in making such an assertion in part because of what might be the single most significant yet under-reported trend in world politics: *The world is significantly more peaceful at the beginning of the twenty-first century than at any time in recorded history*. Although conflict and chaos may dominate the headlines, the incidence of warfare has dropped to remarkably low levels. A far greater percentage of the world's people live in societies at peace than at any other time in history. Not only is the current era markedly better in most measurable categories of international security than ever before, but it is growing more stable as time goes by. At the very least, to a growing number of experts, a major clash of arms does not seem plausible. Major war may well have become obsolete.[8] Rather than a "clash of civilizations," a "coming anarchy," or a step "back to the future" toward multipolarity and instability, the new century may well prove to be far more peaceful than any previous ones.

The number and intensity of *all kinds of conflict*, including interstate wars, civil wars, and ethnic conflicts, declined steadily throughout the 1990s and into the new decade.[9] This period of peace may be due to some combination of nuclear weapons, complex economic interdependence, the spread of democracy, or, as many scholars believe, a simple change in ideas about what is worth fighting for. These days, not much may be left.

This rather bold and perhaps counterintuitive claim may seem a bit utopian to those familiar with the long, dismal history of warfare. Is not war an innate part of human nature, an outgrowth of our passions and imperfections, like murder? Not necessarily, say many of the scholars. After all, murder is an act of the individual, often of passion rather than reason; war is a rational act of state, a symptom of the broader practices of the international system of states. War is an institution, a tradition of dispute resolution, a method countries have chosen to employ when their interests diverge. Granted, it has been with us since the beginning of time, but as political scientist John Mueller has noted, "unlike breathing, eating or sex, war is not something that is somehow required by the human psyche, by the human condition, or by the forces of history."[10] The eminent military historian John Keegan reports being "impressed by the evidence that mankind, wherever it has the option, is distancing itself from the institution of warfare."[11] If Keegan is impressed, then maybe we should be, too.

Overall, as the table below shows, international and internal conflict has steadily declined since the end of the Cold War. Despite perceptions that the current wars "on terror" and in Iraq may have created, the world is a much safer place than it was in prior generations. There remains a human (and perhaps particularly American) tendency to replace one threat with another, to see international politics as an arena of dangerous competition, but this perception simply no longer matches the facts.

The evidence is apparent on every continent. At the beginning of 2008, the only conflict raging in the entire western hemisphere was the ongoing civil war in Colombia, but even that was far less severe than it was a decade ago. Europe, which of course has been the most war-prone of continents for most of human history, was

## Trends in Armed Conflict, 1946–2005

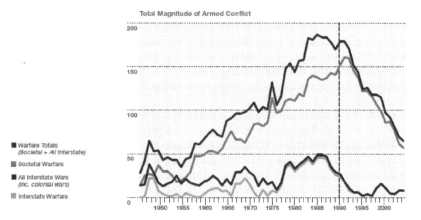

Total Magnitude of Armed Conflict

Warfare Totals
(Societal + All Interstate)

Societal Warfare

All Interstate Wars
(inc. colonial wars)

Interstate Warfare

*Source*: Data used by permission of the Center for International Development and Conflict Management, University of Maryland, College Park. Previously reported by Ted Robert Gurr and Monty G. Marshall, *Peace and Conflict 2005* (College Park, MD: Center for International Development and Conflict Management, 2005), p. 11.

entirely calm, without even the threat of interstate conflict. The situations in Bosnia and Kosovo were not settled, but they were at least stable for the moment. And in contrast to 1914, the great powers have shown no eagerness to fill Balkan power vacuums— to the contrary, throughout the 1990s they had to be shamed into intervention, and were on the same side when they did. The entire Pacific Rim was currently experiencing no armed conflict. Even in the Middle East, where Iraq continued to burn, a tenuous peace was holding between Arabs and Israelis, terrorism notwithstanding, and no other wars seemed imminent.

This trend was even visible in Africa where, despite a variety of ongoing serious challenges, levels of conflict were the lowest they have ever been in the centuries of written history we have about the continent. Darfur and the Congo were the only real extended tragedies still underway; the intensity of the internal conflicts simmering in Algeria, Somalia, Senegal, and a couple of other places is in all cases lower than a decade ago. This can all change quite rapidly—Ethiopia and Eritrea might soon decide to renew their pointless fighting over uninhabitable land, for instance, or Kenya could melt down into chaos—but right now, the continent seems more stable than it has ever been. West Africa is quiet, at least for the moment, as is all of Southern Africa, despite the criminally negligent governance of Robert Mugabe in Zimbabwe.

None of this is to suggest that these places are without problems, of course. But given the rapid increase in world population and number of countries (the League of Nations had 63 members at its peak between the wars, while the United Nations currently has 192), one might expect a great deal more warfare than there currently is. We also are witnessing record low levels of the secondary symptoms of insecurity, such as arms races, military rivalry, and "cold" wars. Either we are merely experiencing another of the world's occasional peaceful periods (and it would be by far the most remarkable such period ever), or something about the nature of international politics has changed, and for the better.

The twentieth century witnessed an unprecedented pace of evolution in all areas of human endeavor, in science and medicine, transportation and communication, and even in religion. In such an atmosphere, perhaps it is not difficult to imagine that attitudes toward the venerable institution of warfare may also have experienced similarly rapid evolution, to the point where its obsolescence could become plausible, even probable, in spite of thousands of years of violent precedent. Perhaps the burden of proof should be on those who say that our rules governing war cannot change, and that it will someday return with a vengeance.

Overall, although the idea that war is becoming obsolete is

gaining ground in academic circles, it has yet to make much headway in those of policymaking. One need not be convinced of its wisdom, however, to believe that *the United States is an extremely safe country*, or at the very least that its basic existence does not depend upon an active presence abroad. No matter what happens in the far corners of the globe, it would seem, America is going to survive the coming century quite well. Even those who most actively support internationalism have a hard time demonstrating that their foreign adventures are truly necessary to assure the basic security of the United States. The benefits of activist strategies must therefore manifestly outweigh the costs, since the United States could easily survive inaction, no matter how dire any future situation appears.

The American people are always told that armed interventions abroad in places like Iraq are emergency operations, necessary to address life-threatening conditions; in reality, because of the low level of threat facing the United States today, they are always elective surgery. And elective surgery, as we all know, often makes problems worse.

## ASSUMPTION #2: INTERNATIONAL ACTIVISM CREATES UNINTENDED CONSEQUENCES, OR "BLOWBACK"

Whether well meaning or not, international activism often complicates the problems faced by the United States. Even the most benign internationalism can result in unintended consequences, popularly known today as "blowback."[12] September 11 was a particularly stark, nasty example. So, while no dire threat compels the United States to actively engage the world, in fact such activism often exacerbates the relatively minor challenges that do still exist.

Divining al Qaeda's motivations is an important task for neo-conservatives seeking to justify their preferred grand strategy. They believe that al Qaeda and its allies attack because of what the United States *is*, rather than what it *does*, which means that restraint would have no effect on the terrorists' level of effort. Despite the fact that bin Laden and his deputy, Ayman al Zawahiri, consistently check off a list of objections to specific U.S. policies, internationalists insist that the main targets of Islamist hatred are modernity, secularism, democracy, and even freedom itself. In one of his periodically released tapes, bin Laden once said that "contrary to Bush's claim that we hate freedom, let him explain why we did not attack Sweden. Clearly those who hate freedom have no pride. We have been fighting you because we are free men who do not remain silent in the face of injustice."[13] Al Qaeda certainly seems to be under the impression that it acts in response to U.S. actions, specifically those propelled by internationalism. Some time ago, the Defense Science Board found a strong correlation between U.S. involvement abroad and terrorist attacks against American targets, and that relationship holds true today.[14] The common belief that terrorism would increase if the United States were to reduce its commitments to the "away game" is therefore completely backwards: If the United States were instead to follow a restrained grand strategy, terrorism against American targets would likely decrease.

Terrorism may be the most prominent form that blowback takes, but it is hardly the only one. Surely it is no coincidence that anti-Americanism abroad has reached record highs during the administration that has veered furthest from a restrained grand strategy.[15] As hard as it is for some people here to believe,

U.S. influence is not universally welcomed. By restraining itself, the United States would declare to the rest of the world that, if left alone, it would respond by leaving the world alone in return. Washington might just discover that anti-Americanism would plummet worldwide if it began to treat other states as adults capable of making their own domestic political and economic choices without patronizing U.S. guidance.

Fortunately, especially in today's nearly post-bellic world, anti-American sentiment is only translated into violence by fringe elements. The Bush administration realized that the best way to undercut that fringe is to decrease anti-American sentiment abroad; as events have amply demonstrated, their means to approaching that end were precisely backwards. Their flawed grand strategy is to blame for the blowback—both violent and peaceful—with which future administrations will have to deal.

## ASSUMPTION #3: MILITARY FORCE IS LESS USEFUL THAN IT USED TO BE

Strategic restraint would not signal the end of U.S. influence in the world, but merely the end of its primary reliance upon "hard power" to accomplish its objectives. Much has been made of the increasing utility of "soft power" in foreign affairs, which political scientist Joseph Nye describes as "the ability to get what we want through attraction rather than coercion or payments."[16] The considerable economic and cultural power of the United States is often far more effective, and certainly less expensive, than its military power.

Contrary to conventional internationalist wisdom, a large military presence abroad is no longer correlated to economic prosperity at home. There exists in some circles a belief, left over from the days of mercantilism, that one of the functions of the military is to look after the economic interests of the state. Although there surely was a time when the great powers engaged in economic warfare and occasionally targeted the financial interests and trade of their rivals, this no longer appears to be the case today. Multinational corporations can generally access the entire world without much fear of undue harassment from host governments, who have strong incentives to provide a healthy, well-regulated atmosphere for investment and trade to flourish. If and when local law enforcement agencies prove incapable of providing protection for the businesses that operate in their territory, modern multinationals surely have the resources either to provide it for themselves, or to move out. In other words, Microsoft does not need the Marine Corps. The United States no longer has to use force to protect its economic interests, since the market can generally take care of itself. Interfering with trade does no country any good. Common interest, not the U.S. military, provides stability for today's globalized economic system.

Military power is also not necessary to advance the ideals of the United States. Strategic restraint need not imply abnegation of our moral responsibility abroad. As events of the last few years have tragically underscored, democracy and freedom are hard to impose on the unwilling. Has the invasion of Iraq—an act that of course seemed wise mainly to the neoconservative advocates of primacy—helped to spread democracy in the Persian Gulf? Recent history provides enough evidence to suggest that the intervention of outside forces tends to exacerbate political instability in places like the Middle East, rather than spread freedom and peace. The United States has always promoted liberty by example far better than it has by force.

## ASSUMPTION #4: THE COSTS OF INTERNATIONAL ACTIVISM FAR OUTWEIGH THE BENEFITS

The best strategy produces maximum benefit for minimum cost. Somewhat surprisingly, cost often seems to be of secondary importance (if that) in most discussions of grand strategy. Since the price of international activism is simply staggering, basic economic rationality would suggest that the benefits ought to be commensurate. Rather than address what deserves to be a central issue, activist strategists often merely ignore cost altogether, or make counterfactual arguments about the exorbitant costs of *not* spending hundreds of billions abroad.

There is probably little need to dwell upon the litany of domestic problems facing the United States, from poverty to health care to Social Security. Warnings from economists about the danger posed by the booming deficit often seem to be ignored by policymakers. The nation remains criminally unprepared for predictable disasters, as Hurricane Katrina made painfully clear. More than $3 trillion has been or will be spent because of Iraq, while chemical plants remain unconscionably unprotected. First responders are woefully underfunded and undertrained. Little slack exists in a health care system that is unprepared to face a major emergency. Port security officials only have the resources to inspect 2 percent of the cargo containers entering the United States. Overall, the "war on terror" has been an enormous drain on the national treasury for what may prove to actually be a net negative benefit to the security of the nation. Today, internationalism gives a priority to imagined threats abroad instead of the real, measurable risks at home. One wonders why the American people have not yet risen as one and demanded restraint.

As a broad rule of thumb, the United States spends approximately three times what it needs to be safe. America would be just as secure if it spent less than 2 percent of its GDP on its military, not between 3 and 4 where it is today. The benefit of any additional spending is diminished by the law of marginal returns: There comes a point where money supposedly spent to address security concerns ceases to make us more safe. If we were to spend twice as much as we do now, for instance, we will not be twice as safe; if we spend half, we will not be half as safe. Security is not an arithmetical asset, one whose presence is directly related to how much is spent. Iceland spends almost nothing on its defense, but it is no less safe.

The rest of the world seems to have grasped this already. In fact, a brief scan of the horizon reveals that all but one of the world's largest countries seems to have determined that addressing the challenges of the twenty-first century does not require enormous military spending and international engagement. The United States spends more on its military than the rest of the world combined. Once Great Britain maintained a "two navy standard," which kept the Royal Navy at least as big as the next two competitors combined; today, the U.S. Navy is maintaining what is in effect a *seventeen* navy standard, a level bigger than at least the next seventeen navies (many of which are among our closest allies).[17] While the other great powers of the world seem to favor already a restrained grand strategy, the United States races ahead, alone.

# Risks

Restraint's skeptics have attacked in three quite predictable ways: The stability of the world would be in jeopardy if the United States restrains itself, we are told. In addition, we have moral obligations to help our fellow human beings. This might be thought of as the *Spider-Man* objection, for in that movie a young Peter Parker receives sage advice from his uncle: "With great power comes great responsibility." Finally, people tend to think that "history shows" that restraint doesn't work. As the arguments below should demonstrate, these objections fundamentally misunderstand either restraint or the nature of the twenty-first-century international system.[17]

## STABILITY

Would global anarchy follow a cutback of U.S. military spending? Were the United States to abandon its commitments abroad, argued political scientist Robert Art, "the world will become a more dangerous place and, sooner or later, that will redound to America's detriment."[19] The eminent historian Arthur M. Schlesinger, Jr., felt that restraint would mean "a chaotic, violent, and ever more dangerous planet."[20]

During the 1990s, the United States under President Clinton experimented with restraint in a very limited way, cutting back its defense spending to a small degree. By 1998, the United States was spending $100 billion less on defense in real terms than it had in 1990.[21] To internationalists and defense hawks, this irresponsible "peace dividend" endangered both national and global security. "No serious analyst of American military capabilities," argued neoconservative intellectuals William Kristol and Robert Kagan, "doubts that the defense budget has been cut much too far to meet America's responsibilities to itself and to world peace."[22] Much to their surprise, no doubt, the world grew *more peaceful* throughout the 1990s while the United States cut its forces. No state seemed to believe that its security was endangered by a less capable United States military, or at least none took any action that would suggest such a belief. No militaries were enhanced to address power vacuums; no security dilemmas drove insecurity or arms races; no regional balancing occurred once the stabilizing presence of the U.S. military was diminished. The rest of the world acted as if the threat of international instability and war was not really a pressing concern, despite the reduction in U.S. military capabilities. The hegemon did not need to maintain international stability.

This evidence from the 1990s is not sufficient to make any kind of definitive connection between the cuts in the U.S. defense budget and continued international stability, of course. One could easily argue that it was the U.S. foreign political and security commitments that maintained stability throughout the decade, not the size of its military, and since those commitments were not significantly altered during this period, instability should not have been expected. However, if the opposite had occurred, if other states had reacted to news of cuts in U.S. defense spending with more aggressive or insecure behavior, then surely that would be cited by internationalists as proof of the wisdom of their strategy. As it stands, the only evidence that we have about the probable international reaction to a restrained United States suggests that the rest of the world can actually operate quite effectively without the presence of a global policeman. As my Naval War College colleague and Africa expert Steve Emerson has said, it seems that in many places there are regional "neighborhood watches" that render the cops from the United States superfluous. Either way, there is reason to believe that U.S. restraint would not destabilize the rest of the world. Those who think otherwise base their view on faith alone.

Were America to become more restrained, nuclear weapons would still affect the calculations of the would-be aggressor; the process of globalization would continue, deepening the complexity of economic interdependence; and democracy would not shrivel where it currently exists. Most important, the idea that war is a worthwhile way to resolve conflict would have no reason to return. Strategic restraint in such a world would be virtually risk-free.

## MORALITY

Perhaps the United States would be ignoring a host of moral and humanitarian obligations by retreating behind secure walls. America is after all the "indispensable nation," according to Madeleine Albright, the benign hegemon, the leading moral actor in a chaotic world. Were the United States to abandon its commitment to humanity, it would not only be committing a sin of omission, but it would also be forfeiting an unprecedented chance to make the world into a better place. "America has the capacity to contain or destroy many of the world's monsters," argued Kristol and Kagan. "A policy of sitting atop a hill and leading by example becomes in practice a policy of cowardice and dishonor."[23]

However, only the most restrictive definition of restraint (isolationism) would preclude Washington from shouldering its fair share of global humanitarian burdens. No serious proponent of restraint has ever argued that the United States has any excuse to shirk its international responsibilities. Jefferson was "willing to hope, as long as anybody will hope with me, that free institutions would peacefully establish a foothold even in the most highly fortified footholds of despotic power."[24] Even Senator Robert A. Taft, who was one of the most prominent post–World War II opponents of internationalism, wrote: "I don't mean to say that, as responsible citizens of the world, we should not gladly extend charity or assistance to those in need. I do not mean to say that we should not align ourselves with the advocates of freedom everywhere. We did this kind of thing for many years, and we were respected as the most disinterested and charitable nation in the world."[25] Restraint does not imply indifference to the world's problems, any more than internationalism automatically implies concern.

Strategic restraint merely rejects the notion that the United States has the sole responsibility to police the world, a national *noblesse oblige* that it alone can address. It is logical and reasonable that the United States, as the world's richest country, should be called upon to make the largest contributions to multilateral institutions. Restraint merely provides two counsels about humanitarian and developmental assistance: First, that their burdens should be shared and performed in conjunction with the other wealthy nations of the industrialized world; and second, that they should not be conflated with security or political aid. Foreign humanitarian assistance is cheap, relatively speaking, and often carries benefits for donor and recipient alike.

Restraint would not demand an abandonment of idealistic ends for the United States, merely an alteration of the means used to pursue them. The founding fathers certainly believed that U.S. ideals are best promoted by example, not by force; they understood that the United States was as much an idea as a country, a political theory as much as reality. The "shining city on the hill" of the Puritan imagination provided a beacon of light, and inspiration for aspiring democrats everywhere. Its military did not need to come down off that hill for it to be a strong ally of freedom and justice throughout the world. The potential power of that example is still quite strong, and the wisdom of the founders is still worth heeding.

## HISTORY

Does "historical experience" demonstrate that the United States cannot remain disengaged from the world for long? The twentieth century seems to provide evidence to believe that when restraint rears its ugly head in the United States, the rest of the world deteriorates into anarchy. The two world wars supposedly taught future American grand strategists two lessons: First, that without active U.S. involvement, the Old World will descend into chaos; and second, that it is an illusion to believe that the United States will be able to remain aloof from such chaos. Therefore, it is in the interest of the United States to remain actively engaged in Eurasia in order to prevent the kind of major conflagration in which it will inevitably become involved. The United States should only embark upon a restrained path if it is prepared to risk fighting the next world war. While it is not clear that either of these "lessons" was ever very valuable, there can be little doubt that they have virtually nothing to teach us today.

It deserves to be recalled that the United States managed to stay out of every European war between 1776 and 1917, and could have certainly stayed out of World War I without much danger. It was Woodrow Wilson's crusading internationalism (and the fact that many in this country, like Teddy Roosevelt, thought that it was dishonorable and unmanly *not* to engage in every war possible), not vital national interest, that sent American troops "over there." At the time, and for years afterward, this was a very controversial decision, to say the least. The desire for restraint, and "normalcy," led the American people to reject Wilsonianism decisively in 1920, in one of the most lopsided elections in American history.

It is quite a stretch to suggest that a more internationalist U.S. grand strategy could have prevented either the Japanese or the German quest for empire in the years that followed. In fact, the entire premise is a bit of a puzzle. The United States was battling depression throughout the 1930s, and was hardly in a position to intervene in Europe in order to stiffen French and British back-bones at Munich. If Roosevelt had demanded a seat at that 1938 conference and refused to cede Czechoslovakia to Hitler, would that have somehow ended the Führer's desire for power and revenge against the Allies? Perhaps internationalists would have counseled Uncle Sam to intervene earlier, in an attempt to influence the outcome of the German election of 1933 that brought the Nazis to power? Or should it have poured money into the Weimar Republic in hopes of staving off its economic implosion? In other words, it is not at all clear how the United States could have prevented the rise of Hitler, or tempered his ambitions. In hindsight, it seems like we should have "done something," but what exactly that would have been is not at all obvious. Europe was on the road to war, no matter what strategy the United States followed.

In the Pacific, the lessons are even less clear. The road to Pearl Harbor was not paved with American inattention or restraint, but with its *active opposition* to Japanese expansion. Throughout the 1930s, Japan had imported nearly all of its oil from the United States. In the summer of 1941, the Roosevelt administration, horrified by Tokyo's actions on the Asian mainland, cut off that supply. The Japanese quickly became desperate, seizing the oil deposits of the Dutch East Indies and attacking the American fleet at Pearl Harbor on December 7 of that year. A good case can of course be made that the embargo was the correct decision, since that oil was being used to fuel the Japanese war machine that was raping Chinese cities. Still, the point remains that strategic restraint can hardly be blamed for dragging the United States into the war in the Pacific, since the United States was steadily taking a more consistent pro-China stance, and acting accordingly. Presumably Tokyo would have had no reason to strike a genuinely neutral United States.

The experience of World War II ought instead to teach a quite different lesson. The great powers of the Old World fought each other to the point of exhaustion, but because the United States had the wisdom to remain neutral for more than two years, it escaped the worst of the suffering. Although nearly three hundred thousand Americans lost their lives in combat, the United States was the only major participant that emerged from the war stronger, in both relative and absolute terms. During the war, American wages increased 68 percent, while the cost of living increased only 23 percent.[26] A very good case can be made that restraint actually served the nation quite well, or as well as could be hoped amid great tragedy.

The United States should not and indeed could not have stayed out of World War II, which was both a geopolitical challenge and a rather clear moral crusade that rid the world of a powerful menace. However, world wars are unlikely ever to occur again, and even if they do, the United States will always have the option to stay out of them. If instability and war were to return to Eurasia, American involvement is hardly inevitable. History provides many examples of states bordering great powers at war that seem to manage to remain on the sidelines, which is presumably even easier to do when there is an ocean in the middle.[27] Wars are rational choices of state, not forest fires that engulf both willing and unwilling bystanders.

During the Cold War, there was an identifiable challenge to U.S. interests. If the Soviet Union had managed to spread communism around the world, the United States would have been threatened in at least three ways. The first of these, the military threat, was probably the least pressing, since as long as the United States maintained its nuclear arsenal outright conquest remained all but impossible. The other two threats—political and economic—were more realistic. The precarious balance that any democracy faces between liberty and security would have tilted decisively toward the latter if the United States had found itself alone in a hostile world. It is difficult to imagine how American democracy could have long survived as an island in a totalitarian sea. It was therefore imperative for the United States to oppose the spread of communism in Eurasia, for the very survival of liberty might have been at stake. American prosperity would also have been in danger if the rest of the world had been swept into the Communist camp, because embargoes and blockades could have wrecked the U.S. economy and devastated the standard of living. Internationalism thus made some limited sense during the Cold War, when domination of Eurasia by an unfriendly power could have resulted in very real political and economic consequences for the West. It is understandable why restraint was not a very popular grand strategy while the Soviet Union was actively attempting to undermine the United States.

That conflict came to a merciful end nearly two decades ago, but for some reason high levels of international engagement continued. Great power conflict today is all but unthinkable; therefore, calculations surrounding the dangers posed by a united Eurasia should change, since the threats it once posed no longer exist. A conventional military threat, which was never overly realistic, today borders on preposterous. More important, the collapse of Communist authoritarianism has left no political alternative to democracy, and no economic alternative to free markets.[28] Although totalitarianism persists in some regions of the world, true political legitimacy in today's international society comes from a mandate from the masses. Even if democracy does not soon sweep across these last bastions of illiberalism (although it just might), it is certainly not losing ground to any other forms of government. No political ideology exists around which to rally a hostile coalition of states against the major democratic powers . Freedom and liberty in the United States are safe.

Islamic fundamentalism hardly poses a threat equivalent to communism or fascism, despite the far right's attempts to equate bin Laden with Stalin and Hitler. Americans fighting the "long war" are told that the goal of al Qaeda's grand strategy is to reestablish the fourteenth-century Islamic Caliphate, uniting all Muslim land from Morocco to Indonesia under one ruler. Few people seem to have noticed, however, that such an outcome lies somewhere between remarkably unlikely and impossible. One might be hard-pressed to explain exactly what kind of material threat a "caliphate" would pose in the first place; but for now, it should be sufficient to note that it is not going to come about. To the extent that they can be considered strategists at all, al Qaeda's leaders are extremely poor at matching ends with means. Overall, fundamentalist Islam hardly poses the kind of threat that communism did, if only because its potential appeal is limited to the Muslim world, and even there it has not proven to be very popular. If anything, the fundamentalist movement is even weaker today than it was on 9/11.

In addition, although the flavors may differ, free market capitalism is almost universally recognized as the fastest route to prosperity and wealth. Even if a group of unfriendly governments came to power in Eurasia, they would still find it in their interest to maintain trade relations with the United States. No country would determine that cutting ties to the world's largest market and producer of goods would be in its interest. As long as capitalism remains the dominant form of economic organization on earth—and there is not much evidence suggesting that any change is on the horizon— the danger from a hostile, mercantilist coalition on the Eurasian landmass is extremely low. In fact, since when the U.S. economy is weak the whole world suffers, most nations today have a vested interest in helping to sustain positive growth in the United States.

Overall, one need not be convinced that the United States should have been restrained at all times in its history to be convinced that it is the wisest course now. In his famous warning about entangling alliances, Washington made exceptions for emergencies, arguing that temporary alliances will occasionally have to be made until storms pass. The Cold War was just such an emergency, and now that it has ended, so should our temporary engagement.

The extraordinary capacity of the United States to respond to emergencies is the most important and overlooked lesson from twentieth-century history, rather than the misplaced and anachronistic analogies to unique crises. Prior to both world wars, the United States maintained a small standing military; by their end, it had produced the best the world had to offer. The numbers for World War II appear in the table below.

In 1941, U.S. automakers produced 3 million cars; during the entire duration of the war, following their transition to military production, they produced just 139. But by war's end, the Ford Motor Company was producing one B-24 bomber every sixty-three minutes.[29] The United States entered World War II with a relatively small military-industrial base; it ended it with the finest in the world.

Today, despite the increased complexity of some of the systems the military employs, overall the United States maintains the potential to surge to meet any imaginable threat. Internationalists seem curiously unwilling to place trust in the ability of the United States to respond if and when crises arise, acting instead as if restraint would permanently neuter the nation and leave it vulnerable to any number of future challenges. In reality, if the worst-case scenarios of the neoconservative imagination were ever to come to pass, the United States would have plenty of time to

HISTORIC SURGE CAPACITY OF THE UNITED STATES

|  | 1939 | 1945 |
|---|---|---|
| U.S. Army | 175,000 | 8,300,000 |
| U.S. Navy | 150,000 | 3,320,000 |
| U.S. Marine Corps | 28,000 | 470,000 |

U.S. population, 1940: 133 million

U.S. population, 2006: 300 million

Source: Population statistics from the U.S. Census; military statistics compiled from official histories of World War II. See also Murray and Millett, *A War to Be Won.*

react and adjust its strategy accordingly. The oft-demonstrated ability of this country to rise to meet serious challenges brewing overseas is the ultimate insurance policy against national catastrophe. Instead of having faith in that insurance, however, the Bush administration chose to invest heavily in preventive measures. Sometimes this can be a prudent policy; but when those catastrophes are extraordinarily unlikely, preventive policies are an illusion, one that fundamentally misunderstands the causes of international stability. This illusion encourages activist policies which may not always be harmful in themselves, since they do not make great power war more likely. They are merely expensive ventures in pointlessness.

By insisting on remaining prepared for all contingencies, plausible and implausible, the United States squanders the greatest gift bestowed by geography: time. Not only is a sneak attack impossible outside the world of science fiction, but today no large-scale military buildup can be accomplished without our knowledge. Should there come a time when a great power or coalition of powers decides to make atavistic strategic choices, the United

States will be able to react in due course. Most security challenges in the modern world need not be addressed immediately. And it is useful to keep in mind that the worst-case scenarios are highly unlikely in the first place, given the trends in twenty-first-century international security. Since minor contingencies often burn themselves out, given enough time, delay can often prove to be advantageous.

In 1803, Jefferson wrote that "we should be most unwise, indeed, were we to cast away the singular blessings of the position in which nature has placed us, the opportunity she has endowed us with of pursuing, at a distance from foreign contentions, the paths of industry, peace and happiness."[30] History hardly proves that the United States cannot remain apart from the political events of Eurasia. If anything, experience from the twentieth century suggests that America runs no great risk by generally allowing the Old World to fend for itself.

## Restraint and the "War on Terror"

The debate over grand strategy is not merely an academic exercise carried out in various arcane journals circulating inside a network of insulated ivory towers. As Iraq has made quite clear, the decisions made by strategists have very real, sometimes tragic effects on real-world politics. Choosing the correct grand strategy may be the most important and difficult task facing our leaders, but no strategy has value unless properly implemented. The first step of grand strategic thinking is to identify and prioritize goals, challenges, and interests (ends); the second arranges national resources (means) in pursuit of these goals. I have gone into some detail elsewhere about what a restrained grand strategy would look like in practice.[31] Perhaps it will be sufficient for our purposes here to focus for a moment upon a restrained approach to what is often called the most pressing strategic challenge of our time: Islamic fundamentalist terrorism.

A restrained grand strategy would treat terrorism for what it is: a potentially damaging criminal act, but hardly an existential or strategic threat to the nation. No "war" against it is necessary. The best way to combat terrorism is traditional law enforcement cooperation, which would of course continue unabated no matter what grand strategy the United States chooses to follow. A robust military presence is rarely necessary to aid that enforcement. Terrorism is just one of a host of twenty-first-century transnational security threats that demand multilateral cooperation, coordination, and intelligence sharing. Weapons proliferation, human trafficking, drug smuggling, and piracy are just some of the other such concerns, none of which is particularly amenable to military solutions. It is important (and comforting) to note that there is no meaningful dissension in the industrialized world about how to address the various transnational threats to world order. Cooperation and burden sharing is in the interest of every state. A strategically restrained United States would still be quite active in international law enforcement, and perhaps even more so once these threats are properly classified and resources freed to address such matters. Police action against terrorism is much less expensive than war; it is likely to be far more productive as well.

While we spend time worrying about such events, a moment's perspective is in order: Diplomats of all prior ages would have been quite grateful to have our problems. People of any previous generation would gladly have traded places with those whose major security threats are terrorists, failing states, rogue states, drugs, and global warming. The current era is not without its dangers, of course, but *our responses to those dangers should be proportional.* Most of what we face are second-order threats, and they do not necessitate first-order spending to be properly addressed.

IN THE FALL OF 2007, Thomas Friedman, who was a strong supporter of the war in Iraq at its outset, wrote in the *New York Times* that he had come to the conclusion that "9/11 has made us stupid. I honor, and weep for, all those murdered on that day. But our reaction to 9/11—mine included—has knocked America completely out of balance, and it is time to get things right once again."[32] The way to begin to do this, and to put this country on the road to recovery after Iraq, is to follow a grand strategy of strategic restraint.

Basic logic suggests that the United States ought to expend the minimum amount of its blood and treasure while seeking the maximum return on its investment. Activism is justified only when there is clear necessity; our default option ought to be *not* to engage. Most of the time, when crises arise, we would be better off if we turned an old maxim on its head: Don't just do something, America, stand there. The United States ought not be heavily involved abroad merely because it *can*, but only because it *has to* (or, to the idealist, because it *should*). In other words, there are only two reasonable justifications for internationalism: to address threats or to pursue opportunities. In today's world, the threats are minimal, and the pursuit of those opportunities is not aided by a robust military presence.

The specter of restraint seems to hang over the foreign policy community, like a ghost from the past that threatens to rear its powerful, ugly head at any moment. Warnings about its potential resurrection have appeared periodically since World War II, especially following the disasters that inevitably result from muscular internationalism. A spate of warnings followed 9/11, and there is little doubt that the internal enemy will have to be beaten back after the Iraq debacle as well. It is inarguably true that a reservoir of support for our traditional strategy of restraint still exists in the American polity; any leader seeking to lead a change in strategy would have more natural allies than he or she might at first assume. Iraq will no doubt increase their numbers. Within the next couple of years, restraint may well have the two crucial elements necessary for any grand strategy to be implemented: strategic logic and political possibility. Overall, the American public may indeed be ready for restraint, now that it has seen the consequences of the opposite. Like an alcoholic, sometimes a nation must hit rock bottom before it sees the need to make drastic changes. Iraq should be our rock bottom. If the war leads the United States to return to its natural, restrained grand strategy, then perhaps the whole experience will not have been in vain. At this point, this may be the best outcome for which one can hope.

The terrorist attacks of September 11 were obviously a turning point in international politics. But it is not likely that future historians will see them as the declaration of a war on America as much as the beginning of what may turn out to be a period of absurd U.S. foreign policy choices. It's too bad there is no way to charge politicians with strategic malpractice. If there were, the nation would have some legal recourse, a relief for the grieving widows and parents of dead GIs and Iraqi civilians. Instead, the best we can do is to make an honest effort to learn from our mistakes, and pledge to future generations that we will try not to repeat them.

# Conclusion

## TO END A WAR

*The difficulty with us is making peace. Every fool can pick a quarrel*
*but I do not remembr any Minister wise enough to end a war.*

—LORD GEORGE GERMAIN,
who was to become Secretary for America, prior
to the outbreak of hostilities in the New World[1]

How wars end can often be more important than how they
begin. A good ending, to the extent that such things are
possible, can minimize suffering and provide a strong foundation
for a just, stable peace. A bad ending, one that is not accepted by
some or all of the participants, may lead to a number of unpleasant
complications and in worst cases can make future conflict likely.
The war in Iraq was begun needlessly and executed poorly, but it
still has the chance to end well. The final act in Iraq has yet to be
written. The way this war concludes will go a long way in determining the extent of the difficulty that the American people will
have in traveling through the four stages toward ultimate recovery. Fortunately, many countries have been in our position before,
and there are lessons to be learned from their experiences. We
can turn for a final time to the Spanish efforts to pacify the revolt
of the Dutch and to the English war against the rebel American

colonists for clear, contrasting examples of how—and how not—
to end unsuccessful wars.

## Ending Wars

"The war in the Netherlands," observed an adviser to Philip IV of
Spain in 1623, "has been the total ruin of this Monarchy."[2] The
struggle to put down the rebellion in their northern provinces
had at that point been raging for fifty-six years, at enormous cost
to the Spanish in blood and treasure. In the same speech, however, that adviser recommended a renewal and intensification of
the effort to subdue the Dutch. Financial ruin and the loss of the
imperial power were apparently small prices to pay to avoid having to admit humiliation and defeat. The Spanish were to go on
bleeding for another thirty-six years; afterwards, the Hapsburg
Empire, which had been the greatest the world had ever seen, was
never the same. A series of Spanish kings therefore chose to sacrifice their empire in the boggy Low Countries of the Netherlands
rather than accept defeat.

A century and a half later, when what was then the greatest empire in the world faced a similar revolt in an imperial
province, the outcome was far different. We sometimes forget
that Yorktown did not have to spell the end of the American
Revolution. After all, in 1781 the British still held a number of
strategically important parts of the rebellious colonies, including
New York, Charleston, and Rhode Island, and had approximately
thirty thousand troops stationed over there. They could have easily just chalked the defeat up to the surprise intervention of the
French fleet, reinforced the remaining troops, and fought on.

George III and his local commander, Lord Cornwallis, wanted to do just that, and showed no interest in granting independence to the traitorous colonists. An enormously contentious parliamentary debate ensued, one which employed much of the same rhetoric as all debates over defeat. The king was convinced that with perseverance and courage the war could be won. "With the assistance of Parliament," he wrote to his ministers, "I do not doubt a good end may yet be made of the war. If we despond, certain ruin ensues."[3] According to the king, the British needed to stay the course.

Fortunately for the British Empire (and for the colonies), the anti-war faction won the debate. The famous historian and member of Parliament Edward Gibbon, who was a strong supporter of the war at its outset, expressed the view of many. "I shall never give my consent," he said, "to exhaust still further the finest country in the world in this prosecution of a war from whence no reasonable man entertains any hope of success. It is better to be humbled than ruined."[4] The government of Lord North crumbled; Whigs came to power, under Lord Rockingham, with the expectation that they would put an end to the war. Yorktown was the turning point in the effort to repress the rebellion. The British admitted defeat—or perhaps more accurately, they admitted that the war was no longer worth the cost—and pulled their troops out.

By all measurable indicators, the British emerged from the debacle stronger than before. In the war's aftermath, the power of the Parliament, and therefore of the people, increased over that of the sovereign, advancing the power of British democracy. The volume of Anglo-American trade actually increased over what it had been before the war.[5] As is usually the case, the prewar predictions that the British Empire could not survive the loss of the American colonies proved to be false. Quite to the contrary, its glory years still lay ahead.

When faced with near-certain defeat, the wise cut their losses and regroup to fight another day. We ought to keep in mind that there is no natural limit to the amount of America's resources, or to the number of its children, that can be sacrificed in Iraq. The great desert quagmire will happily absorb whatever we throw at it, for as long as we decide to stay. An act of political bravery, one demanding far more courage than it took to begin the war in the first place, will be required to bring it to an end. All historical experience suggests that the sooner that happens, the better off all sides will be. At the very least, it will allow the American people to begin to recover from this war, and get past the initial, more destructive stages of development after defeat.

General Petraeus told congressional delegations in the fall of 2007 that in a decade the violence should have dwindled to a manageable level.[6] That is almost certainly true, whether the United States pulls its troops out or not. Eventually, inevitably, the violence in Iraq will wane. The refugee flow will slow to a trickle, and reverse itself; the internecine violence and ethnic cleansing in Baghdad will drop to manageable levels. There will come a point when all the people with the inclination and the means to flee from Iraq will have done so. The people of Baghdad, and those who return home from abroad, will segregate themselves into defensible enclaves, and create de facto partition lines throughout the capital. The death squads will run out of people to kill. Iraqis will rest, if only to reload. No matter what the United States does, peace will eventually come to Mesopotamia. Optimists can believe that its arrival is already not too far away.

All civil wars end. Oftentimes the end comes due to exhaustion and attrition as much as anything else, but end they do. So too will this civil war, whether or not Americans are standing between the guns. The arrival of that day will probably be postponed, not hastened, by the presence of U.S. troops. One of the most influential historians of Vietnam concluded that the United States "prolonged for as much as 20 years a war that might have ended much earlier, with losses of human lives that ran into the millions."[7] It is still within our capability to avoid a tragic repetition in Iraq.

The United States cannot set off down the path toward recovery and national reconciliation before the war in Iraq comes to a conclusion. For this and many other reasons, this nation should put the war's end high on its list of national priorities. That list, however, has been profoundly skewed for quite some time.

## Iraq and Our Priorities

One of the crucial functions of any grand strategy is to prioritize national goals. Its policies are in some senses a reflection of what a government holds dear, of how it sees its function and its relationship to the world and its own people. In the end, all budget decisions reflect the priorities that the government identifies. Throughout its tenure in office, the Bush administration's priorities were blindingly obvious, and its "freedom agenda" (which included the war in Iraq) was executed at the expense of domestic goals. Every dollar that was borrowed and spent in Iraq was one that was unavailable for other needs. Time and time again, internationalists have proven more than willing to let the homeland rot while they tilt at foreign windmills.

The misplaced priorities of the current grand strategy could not have been made more clear than at the end of the summer of 2005. Hurricane Katrina was the most expensive engineering disaster in our nation's history. No matter what the common impression may be, it was *not* a natural disaster, at least not in Louisiana. While coastal Mississippi felt the wrath of God, the people of New Orleans suffered from the incompetence of the Army Corps of Engineers. FEMA became the target of national rage that would have been better directed at the criminally incompetent Corps, whose mistakes led to the death of nearly two thousand people and the destruction of hundreds of thousands of homes.

Unfortunately for New Orleans, the Corps was not working for al Qaeda (so far as we know). Since the destruction of the city (and, in the interests of full disclosure, my home) was due to engineering incompetence rather than terrorist malice, no national priority has been placed on rebuilding. A grand strategy based upon strategic restraint would help America reorient its national priorities, and prevent such abject travesties from recurring. Before bringing freedom, justice, and safety to far corners of the globe, perhaps we should first assure that they exist at home.

Protecting a city the size of New Orleans from future floods is not a particularly difficult task. The Dutch protect their entire country, all of which lies under the level of the sea. The science is rather uncontroversial, and the engineering straightforward. The first step is to construct sturdy levees that can withstand category five storms. Next, a few rather sizable regional projects would make the fix complete: Redirect a portion of the Mississippi to restore the wetlands, and close the Mississippi River Gulf Outlet, which acts as a convenient funnel for the sea's invasions. The total price tag for these tasks would be around $30 billion, spread over ten years, which is roughly what is pumped into Iraq every two months.[8] How we can accept a situation where our money flows more smoothly to rebuild Baghdad than New Orleans is a puzzle to those who live on the Gulf Coast, and ought to create more outrage nationwide than it has to this point.

There is obviously a long list of national projects that lie unaddressed while we hemorrhage blood and treasure in Iraq. One might deem it rather important to upgrade our transportation infrastructure, for instance, to prevent the occasional catastrophic bridge collapse. Depending on one's political persuasion, one might think that the hundreds of billions slated for Iraq could be better devoted to a border fence, health care for poor children, missile defense, job training, cancer research, tax cuts, levees, solar power, port security, or even (heaven forbid) paying down the national debt. Senator Joe Biden (D-DE) has said that his father taught him a lesson about priorities: "Don't tell me what you value," the elder Biden used to say, "show me your budget, and I'll tell you what you value." One need not look long at current federal spending to see what the Bush administration has valued, and what it has not. It is little wonder, then, that "change" was the buzzword in the 2008 presidential campaigns of both parties.

Overall, the next few years are likely to be trying ones for the United States. This foolish war has already turned us into a rather pessimistic people, one that seems to be moving beyond the shock and denial stage into anger. Approval ratings for both the president and the Congress dipped to all-time lows in 2007: 82 percent of Americans reported feeling that the world is a more dangerous place than it used to be, and that it is getting worse.[9] A change in the White House will probably help the national mood to some degree, but it is not likely to prove to be a long-term fix. The country is likely to remain starkly divided for decades, right along partisan political lines, no matter who takes office. In such an atmosphere, it will no doubt prove difficult to make major changes in our grand strategy. Politics will, as always, be the enemy of strategy.

As the nation goes through the predictable stages—denial, anger, depression, and acceptance—after this disaster, it will be important for all of us to keep Iraq in perspective. Defeat is going to hurt our pride, our self-image, and our relationship with our leaders; it is going to deepen the surface divisions that exist in this country, gridlocking our politics for a generation. It is going to take years for us (or for our grandchildren) to pay the war's bills. But it is most certainly not going to spell the end of the United States. When the war finally comes to a conclusion, America is not going to be any less safe, prosperous, or powerful. It will be important for us not to let the natural distaste for losing fool us into believing that Iraq was ever important to our national security. Henry Luce of *Time* magazine famously predicted in 1941 that the world was in the beginning of the "American century"; by all tangible and intangible measures, the twenty-first century is likely to be equally American, no matter how events unfold in Iraq.

War may grab the headlines, but violence is simply not a daily fact of life for the vast majority of the people on this planet, and the percentage of those for whom it remains a reality is steadily shrinking. The world is in the midst of an unprecedented era of peace and stability, despite the disruptive efforts of small groups of dangerous fanatics. Terrorists "win" only if civilized society forgets the good news that the last fifteen years have brought. As a rule, the coming century is going to be a significant improvement over its predecessor. The United States will not prove to be an exception to this rule.

# Out of Iraq

There is little point keeping a bandage on a wound that refuses to heal. As everyone knows, there are two ways to remove bandages: One can either proceed slowly, a little at a time, or act quickly and rip it off all at once. The former unnecessarily prolongs the pain and suffering; the latter, while worse in the short term, brings the agony to a quicker end. Only when that bandage is off can the healing process truly begin.

Recovery from the consequences of the Bush administration's strategic blunders cannot begin until the war ends. No one—not Americans, not Iraqis, not anyone—will benefit from an agonizing, drawn-out, Vietnam-like exit. Since there is little reason to believe that Iraq will be more ready to stand on its own in one or two or even ten more years of occupation, there is nothing to be gained by delaying what is now an inevitable U.S. departure. Ripping the bandage off all at once, while frightening and painful, will minimize whatever suffering is on its way. Only when it is off can the United States move into the final stages of post-Iraq recovery.

Elections provide opportunities to change course but no

guarantees that they will be seized. In 1969, newly elected President Nixon was presented with a situation that was similar to the one that will face Bush's successor. Since it was clear to all involved that the war in Vietnam was basically unwinnable, U.S. policy from Tet onward focused on getting out, one way or the other. Nixon and Kissinger insisted that this had to be done "with honor," that no humiliating defeat could be tolerated. They put the country through four more divisive, bloody, and ultimately pointless years. If the United States had withdrawn from Vietnam in 1968, following Senator George Aiken's advice to "declare victory and get out," there is no doubt that the country would have been better off.

Nixon's experience suggests that the initial decisions that our next president makes will prove to be the most strategically influential. Policy decisions have inertia, and tend to stay in place until acted upon by a force. If our course in Iraq is not changed immediately, or is only changed on the margins, then doing so later, once the new administration becomes invested in the war as Nixon's was, will prove to be far more difficult.

That the war was not worth fighting is obvious to most Americans, but it does not yet seem to have penetrated the walls of the Oval Office. There is no way that the current administration will ever change course in Iraq. Like Lyndon Johnson before him, President Bush is too heavily invested in the war, both personally and politically, to see what it is doing to the country. His successor will have the opportunity to reevaluate this war, and to take a fresh look at U.S. interests involved. Perhaps finally U.S. policy in the Gulf, and U.S. grand strategy in general, can be brought into line with our national interests, and with basic common sense.

However severe the domestic consequences of this disastrous war turn out to be, Iraq is destined to be considered a rather inconsequential event in the overall history of international politics. It is a minor war, a tragic sideshow, not a vital battleground in the war against evil. Although it seems to be part of human nature to anticipate disaster, we should keep in mind that no catastrophes are likely to follow our defeat in Iraq. Life will go on; and, apparently unbeknownst to most people, the world will continue to enjoy the greatest period of prolonged peace in its history. Losing the war is going to hurt more than winning it would have felt good, as Sparky used to say, but we should not allow it to alter the fundamental optimism of the United States of America. Our golden ages still lie ahead.

# NOTES

## Introduction

1 Ralph K. White, *Nobody Wanted War* (New York: Doubleday, 1968), esp. pp. 207–75. See also Dominic D. P. Johnson and Dominic Tierney, *Failing to Win: Perceptions of Victory and Defeat in International Politics* (Cambridge, MA: Harvard University Press, 2006), p. 46.

2 Robert Kagan declared the surge to be a success in March—"The 'Surge' Is Succeeding," *Washington Post*, March 11, 2007 p. B7; Charles Krauthammer, in April—"The Surge: First Fruits," *Washington Post*, April 13, 2007, p. A17; and William Kristol gave affirmation in July—"Why Bush Will Be a Winner," *Washington Post*, July 15, 2007 p. B1.

3 For updated statistics on the Iraqi economy, society, security, and political situation, see the *Iraq Index* of the Brookings Institution, maintained by Michael C. O'Hanlon and updated monthly: www.brookings.edu/saban/iraq-index.aspx.

4 The best discussion of the Iraqi economic collapse has been written by *Washington Post* correspondent Rajiv Chandrasekaran, *Imperial Life in the Emerald City: Inside Iraq's Green Zone* (New York: Alfred A. Knopf, 2007).

5 See the Office of the United Nations High Commissioner for Refugees,

"Statistics on Displaced Iraqis Around the World," September 2007, available at www.unhcr.org/cgi-bin/texis/vtx/home/opendoc .pdf?tbl=SUBSITES&id=470387fc2.

6 Bob Woodward, "CIA Said Instability Seemed 'Irreversible,'" *Washington Post*, July 12, 2007, p. A1.

7 Shibley Telhami of the Brookings Institution and the University of Maryland has been tracking the progress of democracy in the Middle East. See his "The Iraq War Has Only Set Back Middle East Reform," National Public Radio, March 14, 2005, available at www.brookings .edu/opinions/2005/0314middleeast_telhami.aspx; and "The Return of the State," *National Interest*, 84 (Summer 2006), pp. 110–14.

8 Susan Page, "Poll: Public Not Swayed by Petraeus," *USA Today*, September 18, 2007.

9 John Mueller of Ohio State University, the leading expert on war and public opinion, makes this point in "The Iraq Syndrome," *Foreign Affairs*, vol. 84, no. 6 (November–December 2005), pp. 44–54.

10 Comments made by Cheney to CNN's Wolf Blitzer on "The Situation Room," January 24, 2007.

11 The classic realist texts include Hans J. Morganthau, *Politics Among Nations: The Struggle for Power and Peace*, 5th ed. (New York: Alfred A. Knopf, 1973), and E. H. Carr, *The Twenty Years' Crisis, 1919–1939* (New York: Harper & Row, 1946). For more recent discussions, see Henry Kissinger, *Diplomacy* (New York: Random House, 1994), and John J. Mearsheimer, *The Tragedy of Great Power Politics* (New York: W. W. Norton, 2001).

12 See the survey of scholars done by Daniel Maliniak, Amy Oakes, Susan Peterson, and Michael J. Tierney, "Inside the Ivory Tower," *Foreign Policy*, 159 (March–April 2007), pp. 62–68.

13 Will Lester, "Poll: Americans Say World War III Likely," Associated Press, July 23, 2005.

14 In April 2007, 82 percent of Americans told pollsters that they felt the world was becoming a more dangerous place, up 3 percent from the year before—Scott Biddle and Jonathan Rochkind, "Anxious Public Pulling Back from Use of Force," *Confidence in U.S. Foreign Policy*

*Index*, 4 (Spring 2007), available at both publicagenda.org and foreign affairs.org.

# Chapter 1

1 Author's interview with Dr. Peter Burns, August 2007.

2 Quoted by Sally Jenkins, "Amid All the Mistakes, Notre Dame's Mystique Lingers," *Washington Post*, October 4, 2007, p. E1.

3 Daniel Kahneman and Amos Tversky, "Prospect Theory: An Analysis of Decision Under Risk," *Econometrica*, vol. 47, no. 2 (March 1979), pp. 263–91.

4 This process is described by the psychologist Barry Schwartz in *The Paradox of Choice: Why More Is Less* (New York: HarperCollins, 2004), chap. 8.

5 Robert Jervis, "Political Implications of Loss Aversion," in Barbara Farnham, ed., *Avoiding Losses/Taking Risks: Prospect Theory and International Conflict* (Ann Arbor: University of Michigan Press, 1994), p. 36.

6 Geoffrey Parker, "Why Did the Dutch Revolt Last Eighty Years?" *Transactions of the Royal Historical Society*, 5th ser., vol. 26 (1976), p. 61.

7 Fred Charles Iklé, *Every War Must End*, 2nd ed. (New York: Columbia University Press, 2005), p. 129.

8 Ralph K. White, *Nobody Wanted War* (New York: Doubleday, 1968), p. 128.

9 John Mueller, *Quiet Cataclysm: Reflections on the Recent Transformation of World Politics* (New York: HarperCollins, 1995), p. 14.

10 Jonathan Rauch, "Will Frankenfood Save the Planet?" *Atlantic Monthly* (October 2003).

11 Marc Siegel, *False Alarm: The Truth About the Epidemic of Fear* (New York: John Wiley & Sons, 2005).

12 Bjorn Lomborg, *Cool It: The Skeptical Guide to Global Warming* (New York: Alfred A. Knopf, 2007), p. 13.

13 The Pentagon study was authored by Peter Schwartz and Doug Randall, "An Abrupt Climate Change Scenario and Its Implications for

United States National Security," October 2003. The staid observer is Colin S. Gray, *Another Bloody Century: Future War* (London: Weidenfeld & Nicolson, 2005), pp. 82–83.

14 *Time*, April 3, 2006.

15 Lomborg, *Cool It*, p. 49.

16 See John Mueller, *Overblown: How Politicians and the Terrorism Industry Inflate National Security Threats, and Why We Believe Them* (New York: Free Press, 2006).

17 Even the people most passionately promoting the term *Islamo-fascism* do not seem to feel that the analogy is very appropriate. David Horowitz, the neoconservative founder of "Islamo-Fascism Awareness Week," which brings fear and loathing to many campuses across the country, told a *National Review* interviewer that one of the reasons he prefers the term is that "in political war which is what the Left has declared on us, it's important to have an emotional label you can stick your enemies with. And it upsets them as well, which is an added fillip." So much for analysis. "Questions and Answers with David Horowitz," *National Review Online*, October 24, 2007.

18. C. Van Woodward, *The Burden of Southern History* (Baton Rouge: Louisiana State University Press, 1968), and James C. Cobb, *Away Down South: A History of Southern Identity* (New York: Oxford University Press, 2005). See also Wolfgang Schivelbusch, *The Culture of Defeat: On National Trauma, Mourning, and Recovery* (New York: Metropolitan Books, 2003), p. 28.

19 Elisabeth Kübler-Ross, *On Death and Dying* (New York: Touchstone, 1997).

20 Schivelbusch, *The Culture of Defeat*, p. 6.

21 "The MACV Commander," *Army Digest*, vol. 22, no. 2 (February 1967), p. 41; William R. Corson, *The Consequences of Failure* (New York: W. W. Norton, 1974), p. 50.

22 George C. Herring, *America's Longest War: The United States and Vietnam, 1950–1975*, 2nd ed. (New York: Alfred A. Knopf, 1973), p. 273.

23 For the quotation and a discussion of the phenomenon, see Schivelbusch, *The Culture of Defeat*, pp. 12–13.

24 For a description, see Stephen Badsey, *The Franco-Prussian War, 1870–1871* (Oxford: Osprey, 2003).

25 Ken Adelman, "Cakewalk in Iraq," *Washington Post*, February 13, 2002, p. A27.

26 Vice President Cheney made the prediction that U.S. forces would be "greeted as liberators" many times, perhaps most prominently on NBC's *Meet the Press*, March 16, 2003.

27 Bob Woodward, *Bush at War* (New York: Simon & Schuster, 2002), p. 81.

28 David Frum and Richard Perle, *An End to Evil: How to Win the War on Terror* (New York: Random House, 2003), p. 114.

29 George J. Andreopoulos and Harold E. Selesky, "Assessing Recovery," in Andreopoulos and Selesky, eds., *The Aftermath of Defeat: Societies, Armed Forces, and the Challenge of Recovery* (New Haven: Yale University Press, 1994), p. 2.

30 New York Supreme Court Justice Thomas Jones, in postwar exile in London, from his *A History of New York During the Revolutionary War*, quoted in Stanley Weintraub, *Iron Tears: America's Battle for Freedom, Britain's Quagmire: 1775–1783* (New York: Free Press, 2005), p. ix.

31 See T. Christopher Jespersen, "Kissinger, Ford, and Congress: The Very Bitter End in Vietnam," *Pacific Historical Review*, vol. 71, no. 3 (August 2002), pp. 439–73.

32 Iklé, *Every War Must End*, pp. 81–82.

33 Daniel L. Wann, Merrill J. Melnick, Gordon W. Russell, and Dale G. Pease, *Sports Fans: The Psychology and Social Impact of Spectators* (New York: Routledge, 2001), p. 172.

34 Ibid. For me, it is not clear that I regain any actual health. In fact there is no fancy psychological term for what usually happens next in my house. We'll have to stick with what my wife calls it: "Twenty Budweisers and dozing off on the couch muttering." Catchy, I think.

35 David Leonhardt and Marjorie Connelly, "81% in Poll Say Nation is Headed on Wrong Track," *New York Times*, April 4, 2008, p. A1.

36 Robert Jervis, "Domino Beliefs and Strategic Behavior," in Robert Jervis and Jack Snyder, eds., *Dominoes and Bandwagons: Strategic*

*Beliefs and Great Power Competition in the Eurasian Rimland* (New York: Oxford University Press, 1991), p. 37.

37 Corson, *The Consequences of Failure*, p. 42.

38 Henry Kissinger, *The White House Years* (Boston: Little, Brown, 1979), p. 197 (emphasis in the original).

39 Christopher Jon Lamb, *Belief Systems and Decision Making in the Mayaguez Crisis* (Gainesville: University of Florida Press, 1989), pp. 68, 72, 73, 81, and 149.

40 Dominic D. P. Johnson and Dominic Tierney, *Failing to Win: Perceptions of Victory and Defeat in International Politics* (Cambridge, MA: Harvard University Press, 2006), p. 2.

41 Quoted by Walter LaFeber, "The Last War, the Next War, and the New Revisionists," *Democracy*, vol. 1, no. 1 (January 1981), p. 96.

42 Norman Podhoretz, "The Case for Bombing Iran," *Commentary* (June 2007).

43 Hedrick Smith, "Reagan: What Kind of World Leader?" *New York Times Magazine*, November 16, 1980.

44 Quoted in Norman Podhoretz, *World War IV: The Long Struggle Against Islamofascism* (New York: Doubleday, 2007), p. 213.

45 Corson, *The Consequences of Failure*, pp. 133–34.

46 Angus Campbell, *The Sense of Well-Being in America: Recent Patterns and Trends* (New York: McGraw-Hill, 1981), p. 164.

47 Gregor Dallas, *1945: The War That Never Ended* (New Haven: Yale University Press, 2005), esp. pp. 164–69.

48 Lawrence James, *The Rise and Fall of the British Empire* (New York: St. Martin's/Griffin, 1994), p. 119; Corson, *The Consequences of Failure*, p. 51.

49 Alistair Horne, *A Savage War of Peace: Algeria 1954–1962* (New York: New York Review Books, 2006), pp. 549, 4.

50 Pastor and pop psychologist Bob Diets explains the reasoning behind this in his best-selling *Life After Loss: A Practical Guide to Renewing Your Life After Experiencing Major Loss*, 4th ed. (Cambridge, MA: Da Capo Press, 2004), p. 53. See also Corson, *The Consequences of Failure*, p. 150.

51 Richard M. Nixon, *No More Vietnams* (New York: Arbor House,

1985), esp. p. 165; Melvin Laird, "Iraq: Learning the Lessons of Vietnam," *Foreign Affairs*, vol. 84, no. 6 (November–December 2005), pp. 22–43.

52 Nixon, *No More Vietnams*.

53 George C. Herring, "The Wrong Kind of Loyalty: McNamara's Apology for Vietnam," *Foreign Affairs*, vol. 74, no. 3 (May–June 1995), p. 154.

54 Robert S. McNamara, *In Retrospect: The Tragedy and Lessons of Vietnam* (New York: Random House, 1995), p. 333.

55 David Halberstam, "McNamara's Mea Culpa Is Too Little, Too Late," *Los Angeles Times*, April 30, 1995, p. J2.

56 "Mr. MacNamara's War," *New York Times*, April 12, 1995.

57 Harry G. Summers, Jr., "Sweet Justice: A Scoundrel Exposed," *Strategic Review*, vol. 24, no. 3 (Fall 1995), p. 52.

58 Schivelbusch, *The Culture of Defeat*, p. 23.

59 Robert Bork, *Slouching Toward Gomorrah: Modern Liberalism and American Decline* (New York: Regan Books, 1996), p. 21.

60 Barbara W. Tuchman, *A Distant Mirror: The Calamitous 14th Century* (New York: Alfred A. Knopf, 1978), p. 483.

61 Jervis, "Political Implications of Loss Aversion," in Farnham, ed., *Avoiding Losses/Taking Risks: Prospect Theory and International Conflict*, p. 28.

62 Iklé, *Every War Must End*, p. 83.

63 Paul Seabury and Alvin Drischler, "How to Decommit Without Withdrawal Symptoms," *Foreign Policy*, 1 (Winter 1970–71), p. 55.

# Chapter 2

1 Michael Geyer, "Insurrectionary Warfare: The German Debate About a Levée en Masse in October 1918," *Journal of Modern History*, vol. 73, no. 3 (September 2001), p. 509.

2 Jeffrey M. Jones, "Satisfaction Ratings Remain in the Doldrums," Gallup Poll, December 14, 2007; the ABC News/*Washington Post* poll discussed in chapter 1 put the number at 74 percent.

3 Ronald Brownstein, *The Second Civil War: How Extreme Partisanship Has Paralyzed Washington and Polarized America* (New York: Penguin Press, 2007).

4 Robin Toner and Jim Rutenberg, "Partisan Divide Exceeds Split on Vietnam," *New York Times*, July 30, 2006, p. A1. John Mueller remarked that "The partisan divide over the war in Iraq is considerably greater than for any military action over the last half-century"—"The Iraq Syndrome," *Foreign Affairs*, vol. 84, no. 6 (November–December 2005), p. 49.

5 John E. Mueller, *War Presidents and Public Opinion* (New York: John Wiley & Sons, 1973), pp. 116–22; and Dominic D. P. Johnson and Dominic Tierney, *Failing to Win: Perceptions of Victory and Defeat in International Politics* (Cambridge, MA: Harvard University Press, 2006), p. 59.

6 Ole R. Holsti and James N. Rosenau, *American Leadership in World Affairs: Vietnam and the Breakdown of Consensus* (Boston: Allen & Unwin, 1984); and George H. Quester, *American Foreign Policy: The Lost Consensus* (New York: Praeger, 1982).

7 Johnson and Tierney, *Failing to Win*, p. 56.

8 See Fredrik Logevall, "First Among Critics: Walter Lippmann and the Vietnam War," *Journal of American-East Asian Relations*, vol. 4, no. 4 (1995), pp. 351–75; Walter L. Hixson, "Containment on the Periphery: George F. Kennan and Vietnam," *Diplomatic History*, vol. 12, no. 2 (April 1988), pp. 149–64; Hans J. Morgenthau, *Vietnam and the United States* (Washington, DC: Public Affairs Press, 1965); and Kenneth N. Waltz, "The Politics of Peace," *International Studies Quarterly*, vol. 11, no. 3 (September 1967), pp. 199–211.

9 A group of thirty-three of the most prominent realists took out an ad opposing the war in the *New York Times* on September 25, 2002. The lone exception is Henry Kissinger, who supported the Iraq crusade from the beginning.

10 Richard M. Nixon, *No More Vietnams* (New York: Arbor House, 1985), p. 209.

11 Ole R. Holsti was one of the first to make this observation in his clumsily

titled, classic article, "The Study of International Politics Makes Strange Bedfellows: Theories of Radical Right and Radical Left," *American Political Science Review*, vol. 68, no. 1 (March 1974), pp. 217–42.

12  Kenneth Boulding et al., *The U.S. and Revolution* (Santa Barbara, CA: RAND Corporation, 1961), p. 5.

13  Holsti and Rosenau, *American Leadership in World Affairs*, p. 249.

14  "Cheney's Law," *Frontline*, October 16, 2007.

15  See Arthur M. Schlesinger, Jr., *The Imperial Presidency* (Boston: Houghton Mifflin, 1973).

16  For a review of Schlesinger's book, see Harvey G. Zeidenstein, "The Reassertion of Congressional Power: New Curbs on the President," *Political Science Quarterly*, vol. 93, no. 9 (Fall 1978), pp. 393–410.

17  See John Lehman, *Making War: The 200-Year-Old Battle Between the President and the Congress Over How America Goes to War* (New York: Scribners, 1992).

18  Joint Resolution of Congress H.J. RES 1145 ("The Gulf of Tonkin Resolution"), August 7, 1964.

19  Quoted in Peter Beinart, "The Isolationist Pendulum," *Washington Post*, January 22, 2006, p. B7.

20  William R. Corson, *The Consequences of Failure* (New York: W. W. Norton, 1974), p. 13.

21  In August 2007, a Gallup Poll found an approval rating for Congress that was the lowest since at least 1974, when such ratings began— Gallup Poll, "Congressional Approval Rating Matches Historic Low," August 21, 2007, available at www.gallup.com/poll/28456/Congress-Approval-Rating-Matches-Historical-Low.aspx.

22  Angus Campbell, *The Sense of Well-Being in America: Recent Patterns and Trends* (New York: McGraw-Hill, 1981), p. 165. For similar polling results, see William Watts and Lloyd A. Free, *State of the Nation 1974* (Washington, DC: Potomac Associates, 1974).

23  Quoted in Gaines M. Foster, "Coming to Terms with Defeat: Post–Vietnam America and the Post-Civil War South," *Virginia Quarterly Review*, vol. 66, no. 1 (Winter 1990), p. 31.

24  See Joseph E. Stiglitz and Linda J. Blimes, *The Three Trillion Dollar*

*War: The True Cost of the Iraq Conflict* (New York: W. W. Norton, 2008), p. 115.

25 See Anthony S. Campagna, *The Economic Consequences of the Vietnam War* (New York: Praeger, 1991).

26 Ibid., p. 134.

27 Otto Eckstein called the failure to enact greater tax increases a "colossal error" on Johnson's part, while noting that most economists are even less forgiving of the decision than he is—Eckstein, *The Great Recession* (New York: North Holland Publishing Co., 1978), p. 26.

28 Stiglitz and Blimes, *The Three Trillion Dollar War.*

29 Ron Suskind, *The Price of Loyalty: George W. Bush, the White House, and the Education of Paul O'Neill* (New York: Simon & Schuster, 2004), p. 291.

30 See the analysis by Ronald Bailey, "Oil Price Bubble?" *Reason Magazine*, March 12, 2008.

31 Neela Banerjee, "Nervous Day in the Pit for Traders of Crude," *New York Times*, March 21, 2003, p. C1.

32 A graphic depiction of this can be found on the U.S. Department of Energy Web site, www.eia.doe.gov/emeu/security/gdpwop.gif.

33 The drug of the day was peyote/mescaline brought from the New World. See Corson, *The Consequences of Failure*, p. 39.

34 Robert Hughes, "Art of Anxiety," *The Guardian*, October 18, 1996,

35 Quoted by Rafael Reuveny and Aseem Prakash, "The Afghanistan War and the Breakdown of the Soviet Union," *Review of International Studies*, vol. 25, no. 4 (October 1999), p. 699. See also Douglas A. Borer, *Superpowers Defeated: Vietnam and Afghanistan Compared* (London: Frank Cass, 1999).

36 Alistair Horne, *A Savage War of Peace: Algeria 1954–1962* (New York: New York Review of Books, 2006), p. 538.

37 The political scientist Colin McInnes makes this observation in *Spectator Sport War: The West and Contemporary Conflict* (Boulder, CO: Lynn Rienner, 2002).

38 The full text of General Sanchez's remarks can be found at www.militaryreporters.org/sanchez_101207.html. His book should be available at a bookstore near you.

39  David Halberstam, *The Powers That Be* (New York: Alfred A. Knopf, 1979), p. 450.

40  Nixon, *No More Vietnams*, p. 162.

41  Corson, *The Consequences of Failure*, p. 45.

42  Robert S. McNamara, *In Retrospect: The Tragedy and Lessons of Vietnam* (New York: Random House, 1995), p. 333.

## Chapter 3

1  President George W. Bush, Remarks on the Fourth Anniversary of Operation Iraqi Freedom, March 19, 2007.

2  For "catastrophic": George F. Will, "America's Moral Duty in Iraq," *Washington Post*, December 4, 2006, p. A19; "disastrous": Glenn Frankel, "The McCain Makeover," *Washington Post Magazine*, August 27, 2006, p. W12; "grave": John McCain, "The War You're Not Reading About," *Washington Post*, April 8, 2007, p. B07.

3  On the enhanced threat perceptions of the United States, see John Mueller, *Overblown: How Politicians and the Terrorism Industry Inflate National Security Threats, and Why We Believe Them*; Robert H. Johnson, *Improbable Dangers: U.S. Conceptions of Threat in the Cold War and After* (New York: St. Martin's Press, 1994); and Frances Fitzgerald, *Way Out There in the Blue: Reagan, Star Wars and the End of the Cold War* (New York: Touchstone Books, 2001).

4  According to two trustworthy sources, a remarkable meeting took place in the White House on January 10, 2003, only two months prior to the invasion. A group of three Iraqi exiles met with President Bush, and were rather surprised, to put it mildly, that he didn't seem to be aware of the Shia/Sunni divide in Islam. The Iraqis told Ambassador Peter Galbraith that "the President was unfamiliar with these terms," and the three "spent part of the meeting explaining that there are two major sects in Islam"—Peter W. Galbraith, *The End of Iraq: How American Incompetence Created a War Without End* (New York: Simon & Schuster, 2006), p. 83. See also George Packer, *The Assassins' Gate: America in Iraq* (New York: Farrar, Straus & Giroux, 2005), p. 96.

I choose not to believe this story. Even though Ambassador Galbraith once told me that he knows two of the three witnesses to this event very well and that they are trustworthy, I find it easier to sleep at night if I simply refuse to believe that the president was unaware of the divide in Islam as he was preparing to send U.S. troops into Iraq. No one could reach the White House without knowing that. Right?

5 Former Ambassador Galbraith has led the charge to beatify the Kurds; see his *The End of Iraq*.

6 For a good review, see Kenneth M. Pollack and Ray Takeyh, "Taking on Tehran," *Foreign Affairs*, vol. 84, no. 2 (March–April 1995), pp. 1–7.

7 Reliable information on military spending can be found in the databases on the Web site of the Stockholm International Peace Research Institute, http://first.sipri.org.

8 Evidently a series of Iranian diplomatic feelers have been sent Washington's way since 9/11, all of which were ignored by the Bush administration, whose neoconservatives refuse to negotiate with evil. See Rupert Cornwell, "Washington Snubbed Iran Offer," BBC News, January 18, 2006; and Gareth Porter, "Burnt Offering," *The American Prospect*, May 21, 2006. More detailed, depressing information was contained in the *Frontline* episode titled "Showdown with Iran," PBS, October 23, 2007.

9 See Scott D. Sagan and Kenneth N. Waltz, *The Spread of Nuclear Weapons: A Debate* (New York: W. W. Norton, 1995).

10 John Mueller, "The Essential Irrelevance of Nuclear Weapons: Stability in the Postwar World," *International Security*, vol. 13, no. 2 (Fall 1988), pp. 55–79.

11 North Korea is the only country to have gained entry to that exclusive "club" since the end of the Cold War. In the same amount of time, South Africa has given up its nuclear weapons, as have Belarus, Ukraine, and Kazakhstan. Fears that uncontrolled proliferation would follow the 1998 Indian and Pakistani tests—which of course merely confirmed a status quo that everyone had been familiar with for years—proved to be predictably unwarranted.

12 See C. J. Campbell, "Running Out of Gas: The Time of the Wolf *Is* Coming," *The National Interest*, 51 (Spring 1998), p. 48.

13 Shibley Telhami, *Power and Leadership in International Bargaining: The Path to the Camp David Accords* (New York: Columbia University Press, 1990), pp. 72–73.

14 For an explanation of oil market dynamics and their relation to political manipulation, see Eugene Gholz and Daryl G. Press, "Energy Alarmism: The Myths That Make Americans Worry About Oil," *Policy Analysis*, 589, April 5, 2007.

15 Henry Kissinger, *Ending the Vietnam War: A History of America's Involvement in and Extrication from the Vietnam War* (New York: Simon & Schuster, 2003), p. 561. See also Shiping Tang, "Reputation, Cult of Reputation, and International Conflict," *Security Studies*, vol. 14, no. 1 (October 2005), pp. 34–62, and Jerome Slater, "The Domino Theory and International Politics: The Case of Vietnam," *Security Studies*, vol. 3, no. 2 (Winter 1993–94), pp. 186–224.

16 George C. Herring, *America's Longest War: The United States and Vietnam, 1950–1975*, 2nd ed. (New York: Alfred A. Knopf, 1973), p. 270.

17 Richard M. Nixon, *No More Vietnams* (New York: Arbor House, 1985), pp. 212–15.

18 Kissinger, *Ending the Vietnam* War, p. 561.

19 Ted Hopf, *Peripheral Visions: Deterrence Theory and American Foreign Policy in the Third World, 1965–1990* (Ann Arbor: University of Michigan Press, 1994), and Johnson, *Improbable Dangers*.

20 Robert Jervis, "Political Implications of Loss Aversion," in Barbara Farnham, ed., *Avoiding Losses/Taking Risks: Prospect Theory and International Conflict* (Ann Arbor: University of Michigan Press, 1994), p. 25.

21 Stephen Biddle, "Seeing Baghdad, Thinking Saigon," *Foreign Affairs*, vol. 85, no. 2 (March–April 2006), p. 5.

22 James Carafano, "What's Next in Iraq? Leaving Too Early Would Help Terrorists," *Des Moines Register*, March 13, 2006, available at the Heritage Foundation Web site, www.heritage.org/Press/Commentary/ed031406a.cfm.

23 William R. Corson, *The Consequences of Failure* (New York: W. W. Norton, 1974), p. 51.

24 See Tom Wicker, "Instead of a Bloodbath," *New York Times*, July 8,

1979, p. E17, and Scott Laderman, "Iraq, Vietnam, and the Bloodbath Theory," *History News Network*, April 10, 2006.

25  President George W. Bush, Remarks at the Veterans of Foreign Wars National Convention, Kansas City, Missouri, August 22, 2007, available at www.whitehouse.gov/news/releases/2007/08/20070822-3.html.

26  For example, Victor Davis Hanson wrote that the Communist victory "brought more death and even greater dislocation to the Vietnamese than did decades of war." Hanson's claims are offered without citation, and seemed to be based on nothing in particular—*Carnage and Culture: Landmark Battles in the Rise of Western Power* (New York: Doubleday, 2001), p. 425.

27  Far right: Norman Podhoretz, *Why We Were in Vietnam* (New York: Simon & Schuster, 1982), p. 198. Far left: Noam Chomsky and Edward Herman, *The Washington Connection and Third World Fascism* (Boston: South End Press, 1979). U.S. Government: Department of State, *1982 Human Rights Report* (Washington, DC: Bureau of Public Affairs, 1983). Journalists: Elizabeth Becker, "Vietnam: The Faltering Revolution," *Washington Post*, September 23, 1979, and Wicker, "Instead of a Bloodbath."

28  Jacqueline Desbarats and Karl D. Jackson, "Vietnam 1975–1982: The Cruel Peace," *Washington Quarterly*, vol. 8, no. 4 (Fall 1985), pp. 169–82.

29  Gareth Porter and James Roberts, "Creating a Bloodbath by Statistical Manipulation," *Pacific Affairs*, vol. 61, no. 2 (Summer 1988), pp. 303–10. The methods used by Desbarats and Jackson, which included interviews of selected refugees, seemed designed to produce a certain outcome. More generally accepted figures put the death toll under ten thousand, in addition to perhaps tens of thousands who drowned during the "boat people" exodus, which in fairness cannot be directly attributed to vengeful North Vietnamese blood lust.

30  For a review of the U.S. relationship with Cambodia in the Vietnam era, see William Shawcross, *Sideshow: Nixon, Kissinger and the Destruction of Cambodia* (New York: Simon & Schuster, 1979).

31  David Shelby, "United States Prepared to Accept Additional Iraqi

Refugees," U.S. Department of State, March 30, 2007; Lionel Beehner, "Iraq's Refugees in Waiting," *CFR Daily Analysis*, April 2, 2007.

32 For more on this strategy, see Edward N. Luttwak, "Iraq: The Logic of Disengagement," *Foreign Affairs*, vol. 84, no. 1 (January–February 2005), pp. 26–36.

# Chapter 4

1 Both the speech and the transcript of the press conference are available in full text on the White House Web page, www.whitehouse.gov. The speech was given on May 23, 2007, and the press conference was on May 24.

2 The president recently told a South Carolina audience that Osama bin Laden "proclaimed that the 'third world war is raging in Iraq.'" The president clearly agrees—George W. Bush, "President Bush Discusses War on Terror in South Carolina," July 24, 2007, available at www .whitehouse.gov/news/releases/2007/07/20070724-3.html, accessed November 13, 2007.

3 George W. Bush, *The National Security Strategy of the United States of America* (Washington, DC: Government Printing Office, 2002), p. 1.

4 Thomas L. Friedman, "Restoring Our Honor," *New York Times*, May 6, 2004, p. A35.

5 A good summary and discussion can be found in "All Iraqi Ethnic Groups Overwhelmingly Reject Al Qaeda" (Washington, DC: World Public Opinion, September 27, 2006), available at www .worldpublicopinion.org/pipa/articles/brmiddleeastnafricara/248 .php?nid=&id=&pnt=248&lb=brme, accessed November 14, 2007.

6 Thomas E. Ricks and Karen DeYoung, "Al Qaeda in Iraq Reported Crippled," *Washington Post*, October 15, 2007, p. A1.

7 Bush, "President Bush Discusses War on Terror in South Carolina."

8 See Stephen Wrage, "Pirates and Parasites," *Washington Post*, October 20, 2001, p. A27; Donald J. Puchala, "Of Pirates and Terrorists: What Experience and History Teach," *Contemporary Security Policy*, vol. 26, no. 1 (April 2005), pp. 1–24; Joseph Wheelan, *Jefferson's War: America's First War on Terror, 1801–1805* (New York: Carroll & Graf, 2003);

Joshua E. London, *Victory in Tripoli: How America's War with the Barbary Pirates Established the U.S. Navy and Shaped a Nation* (New York: John Wiley & Sons, 2005); and Frederick C. Leiner, *The End of Barbary Terror: America's 1815 War Against the Pirates of North Africa* (New York: Oxford University Press, 2007).

9 Quoted by George F. Will, "America's Moral Duty In Iraq," *Washington Post*, December 4, 2006, p. A19.

10 Karen DeYoung and Walter Pincus, "A Qaeda in Iraq May Not Be Threat Here," *Washington Post*, March 18, 2007, p. A20. See also David Froomkin, "They Won't Follow Us Home," *Washington Post Online*, March 19, 2007.

11 One of the few exceptions was the November 2005 bombing of a Jordanian wedding party by the group led by Abu Musab al Zarqawi, which killed fifty-nine people. Although al Zarqawi is a Jordanian, the perpetrators of this attack appear to have included Iraqis. The bombing was a strategic disaster for al Qaeda in Iraq, since it turned Jordanian public opinion against the group, and it has not been repeated.

12 For a discussion, see Ole R. Holsti, "The Study of International Politics Makes Strange Bedfellows: Theories of Radical Right and Radical Left," *American Political Science Review*, vol. 68, no. 1 (March 1974), pp. 217–42.

13 Norman Podhoretz, *World War IV: The Long Struggle Against Islamofascism* (New York: Doubleday, 2007).

14 Newt Gingrich, remarks made on *Fox News Sunday*, July 29, 2007.

15 Newt Gingrich, remarks made on NBC's *Meet the Press*, May 21, 2007.

16 William R. Corson discusses this phenomenon in *The Consequences of Failure* (New York: W. W. Norton, 1974), p. 37.

17 "The Sound of One Domino Falling," *New York Times*, August 4, 2006, p. A16.

18 Quoted and defended by David Frum and Richard Perle, *An End to Evil: How to Win the War on Terror* (New York: Random House, 2003), p. 16.

19 Henry Kissinger, "How to Exit Iraq," *Washington Post*, December 19, 2005, p. B7.

20  Henry Kissinger, "Saving Iraq," *Washington Post*, September 16, 2007, p. B6 (emphasis added).

21  Rich Lowry, "Bush's Vietnam," *National Review*, August 15, 2006.

22  Melvin Laird, "Iraq: Learning the Lessons of Vietnam," *Foreign Affairs*, vol. 84, no. 6 (November–December 2005), p. 36.

23  Newt Gingrich, remarks made on NBC's *The Today Show*, August 7, 2007.

24  Geoffrey Parker, *Spain and the Netherlands, 1559–1659: Ten Studies* (Short Hills, NJ: Enslow Publishers, 1979), p. 53.

25  Robert J. McMahon, "Credibility and World Power: Exploring the Psychological Dimension in Postwar American Diplomacy," *Diplomatic History*, vol. 15, no. 4 (Fall 1991), p. 464.

26  See Hopf, *Peripheral Visions*.

27  Ted Hopf, "Soviet Inferences from Their Victories in the Periphery: Visions of Resistance or Cumulating Gains?" in Robert Jervis and Jack Snyder, eds., *Dominoes and Bandwagons: Strategic Beliefs and Great Power Competition in the Eurasian Rimland* (New York: Oxford University Press, 1991) p. 167.

28  For some representative skepticism about the conventional wisdom, see Jonathan Mercer, *Reputation and International Politics* (Ithaca, NY: Cornell University Press, 1996); Ted Hopf, *Peripheral Visions: Deterrence Theory and American Foreign Policy in the Third World, 1965–1990* (Ann Arbor: University of Michigan Press, 1994); Robert H. Johnson, *Improbable Dangers: U.S. Conceptions of Threat in the Cold War and After* (New York: St. Martin's Press, 1994); and Daryl G. Press, *Calculating Credibility: How Leaders Assess Military Threats* (Ithaca, NY: Cornell University Press, 2005).

29  For a longer, more academic treatment of these ideas, see Christopher J. Fettweis, "Credibility and the War on Terror," *Political Science Quarterly*, vol. 122, no. 4 (Winter 2007–08), pp. 585–615.

30  On North Korea, see the floor speeches of Senator John McCain, such as "The Nuclear Ambitions of North Korea," October 7, 1994, available at www.fas.org/spp/starwars/congress/1994/s941007-dprk.htm, accessed May 22, 2006; on Saddam Hussein, see Eliot A. Cohen,

"Sound and Fury," *Washington Post*, December 19, 1998, p. A25; and Charles Krauthammer, "Saddam: Round 3," *Washington Post*, November 13, 1998, p. A23.

31 Dale C. Copeland, "Do Reputations Matter?" *Security Studies*, vol. 7, no. 1 (Autumn 1997), p. 43.

32 Quoted in John Lewis Gaddis, *Strategies of Containment: A Critical Appraisal of Postwar American Security Policy* (New York: Oxford University Press, 1982), p. 144.

33 Quoted in ibid., p. 240.

34 Steven R. Weisman, "President Appeals Before Congress for Aid to Latins," *New York Times*, April 28, 1993, p. A1.

35 McMahon, "Credibility and World Power," p. 467.

36 Quoted in William M. LeoGrande, "A Splendid Little War: Drawing the Line in El Salvador," *International Security*, vol. 6, no. 1 (Summer 1981), p. 27.

37 Vaughn P. Shannon and Michael Dennis, "Militant Islam and the Futile Fight for Reputation," *Security Studies*, vol. 16, no. 2 (April 2007), pp. 287–317.

38 Laura Egendorf, ed., *Terrorism: Opposing Viewpoints* (San Diego, CA: Greenhaven Press, 1999), p. 125.

39 Henry Kissinger, *The White House Years* (Boston: Little, Brown, 1979), p. 196.

40 Barbara W. Tuchman, *The March of Folly from Troy to Vietnam* (New York: Ballantine Books, 1984), p. 230.

# Chapter 5

1 A very useful review of the various extant definitions of "grand strategy" can be found in Colin Dueck, *Reluctant Crusaders: Power, Culture, and Change in American Grand Strategy* (Princeton, NJ: Princeton University Press, 2006), pp. 9–13.

2 For some of the best discussions of neoconservatives and policy, see Stefan Halper and Jonathan Clarke, *America Alone: The Neoconservatives and the Global Order* (New York: Cambridge University Press, 2004),

and Jacob Heilbrunn, *They Knew They Were Right: The Rise of Neocons* (New York: Doubleday, 2008).

3 See especially John Lewis Gaddis, *Surprise, Security, and the American Experience* (Cambridge, MA: Harvard University Press, 2004), and Robert Kagan, *Dangerous Nation* (New York: Random House, 2006).

4 Eric A. Nordlinger, *Isolationism Reconfigured: American Foreign Policy for a New Century* (Princeton, NJ: Princeton University Press, 1995), p. 4.

5 William R. Corson, *The Consequences of Failure* (New York: W. W. Norton, 1974), p. 155.

6 On the 1970s Committee on the Present Danger, see Ann Hessing Cahn, *Killing Détente: The Right Attacks the CIA* (State College, PA: Penn State Press, 1998); the newer version speaks for itself at www.committeeonthepresentdanger.org.

7 Abraham Lincoln, "The Perpetuation of Our Political Institutions," an Address Before the Young Men's Lyceum of Springfield, Illinois, January 27, 1838, available in Roy P. Basler, ed., *Abraham Lincoln: His Speeches and Writings* (Cambridge, MA: Da Capo Press, 2001), pp. 76–84.

8 See John Mueller, *Retreat from Doomsday: The Obsolescence of Major War* (New York: Basic Books, 1989), and *Quiet Cataclysm: Reflections on the Recent Transformation of World Politics* (New York: HarperCollins, 1995); Richard Rosecrance, *The Rise of the Trading State: Commerce and Conquest in the Modern World* (New York: Basic Books, 1986); Michael Mandelbaum, *Ideas That Conquered the World: Peace, Democracy, and Free Markets in the Twenty-First Century* (New York: Public Affairs, 2002); and Robert Jervis, "Theories of War in an Era of Leading Power Peace," *American Political Science Review*, vol. 96, no. 1 (March 2002), pp. 1–14.

9 See Ted Robert Gurr and Monty G. Marshall, *Peace and Conflict 2005: A Global Survey of Armed Conflicts, Self-Determination Movements, and Democracy* (College Park, MD: Center for International Development and Conflict Management, 2005); Human Security Centre, *Human Security Report 2005* (New York: Oxford University Press, 2005); and Peter

Wallensteen and Margareta Sollenberg, "Armed Conflict, 1989–2000," *Journal of Peace Research*, vol. 38, no. 5 (2001), pp. 629–44.

10 Mueller, *Quiet Cataclysm*, p. 120.

11 John Keegan, *A History of Warfare* (New York: Alfred A. Knopf, 1993), p. 60.

12 Chalmers Johnson, *Blowback: The Costs and Consequences of American Empire* (New York: Henry Holt & Co., 2000).

13 Osama bin Laden, from an audiotape released on October 29, 2004; transcript available on the Web site of the Middle East Media Research Institute, www.memri.org/bin/articles.cgi?Area=sa&ID=SA1404, accessed April 12, 2007.

14 Defense Science Board, *DoD Responses to Transnational Threats* (Washington DC: Office of the Under Secretary of Defense for Acquisitions and Technology, October 1997), p. 15.

15 The Pew Project on Global Attitudes tracks international attitudes, including anti-Americanism; see their reports at www.pewglobal.org/reports.

16 Joseph S. Nye, *Soft Power: The Means to Success in World Politics* (New York: Public Affairs, 2004), p. x.

17 Robert O. Work, *Winning the Race: A Naval Fleet Platform Architecture for Enduring Maritime Supremacy* (Washington, DC: Center for Strategic and Budgetary Assessments, March 1, 2005).

18 A deeper, more academic examination of all the issues in the sections that follow can be found in Christopher J. Fettweis, *Angell Triumphant: The International Politics of Great Power Peace* (New York: Oxford University Press, 2009, forthcoming).

19 Robert J. Art, *A Grand Strategy for America* (Ithaca, NY: Cornell University Press, 2003), p. 11.

20 Arthur M. Schlesinger, Jr., "Back to the Womb? Isolationism's Renewed Threat," *Foreign Affairs*, vol. 74, no. 4 (July–August 1995), p. 8.

21 Michael O'Hanlon, "America's Military, Cut to the Quick," *Washington Post*, August 9, 1998, p. C1.

22 William Kristol and Robert Kagan, "Toward a Neo-Reaganite Foreign Policy," *Foreign Affairs*, vol. 75, no. 4 (July–August 1996), p. 24.

23 Ibid., p. 31.

24 Quoted in Robert W. Tucker and David C. Hendrickson, *The Imperial Temptation: The New World Order and America's Purpose* (New York: Council on Foreign Relations Press, 1992), p. 173.

25 Robert A. Taft, *A Foreign Policy for Americans* (Garden City, NY: Doubleday & Co., 1951), p. 14.

26 See Williamson Murray and Alan R. Millett, *A War to Be Won: Fighting the Second World War* (Cambridge, MA: Harvard University Press, 2000), p. 545.

27 See Eugene Gholz, Daryl G. Press, and Harvey M. Sapolsky, "Come Home America: The Strategy of Restraint in the Face of Temptation," *International Security*, vol. 21, no. 4 (Spring 1997), p. 45.

28 Francis Fukuyama famously (or infamously) made this argument in *The End of History and the Last Man* (New York: Free Press, 1992).

29 Numbers taken from the Ken Burns documentary mini-series *The War*, Episode Two, PBS, September 2007.

30 Quoted in Robert W. Tucker and David C. Hendrickson, *Empire of Liberty: The Statecraft of Thomas Jefferson* (New York: Oxford University Press, 1990), p. 241.

31 Fettweis, *Angell Triumphant*.

32 Thomas L. Friedman, "9/11 Is Over," *New York Times*, September 30, 2007, p. A12.

## CONCLUSION

1 Quoted in Stanley Weintraub, *Iron Tears: America's Battle for Freedom, Britain's Quagmire: 1775–1783* (New York: Free Press, 2005), p. 311.

2 Quoted in Geoffrey Parker, *The Army of Flanders and the Spanish Road, 1567–1659*, 2nd ed. (New York: Cambridge University Press, 2004), p. 227.

3 Weintraub, *Iron Tears*, p. 305.

4 Christopher Hibbbert, *Redcoats and Rebels: The American Revolution Through British Eyes* (New York: W. W. Norton, 1990), p. 334.

5 Lawrence James, *The Rise and Fall of the British Empire* (New York: St. Martin's/Griffin, 1994), p. 119.

6 Shailagh Murray, "After Iraq Trip, Unshaken Resolve," *Washington Post*, August 27, 2007, p. A8.

7 George C. Herring, "The 'Vietnam Syndrome' and American Foreign Policy," *Virginia Quarterly Review*, vol. 57, no. 4 (Autumn 1981), p. 598.

8 Ivor van Heerden and Mike Bryan, *The Storm: What Went Wrong and Why During Hurricane Katrina* (New York: Viking Penguin, 2006), p. 263.

9 Scott Biddle and Jonathan Rochkind, "Anxious Public Pulling Back from Use of Force," *Confidence in U.S. Foreign Policy Index*, vol. 4 (Spring 2007), available at both publicagenda.org and foreignaffairs.org.

# FURTHER READING

BOOKS

Badsey, Stephen. *The Franco-Prussian War, 1870–1871*. Oxford: Osprey, 2003.

Borer, Douglas A. *Superpowers Defeated: Vietnam and Afghanistan Compared*. London: Frank Cass, 1999.

Bork, Robert. *Slouching Toward Gomorrah: Modern Liberalism and American Decline*. New York: Regan Books, 1996.

Brownstein, Ronald. *The Second Civil War: How Extreme Partisanship Has Paralyzed Washington and Polarized America*. New York: Penguin Press, 2007.

Cahn, Ann Hessing. *Killing Détente: The Right Attacks the CIA*. State College, PA: Penn State Press, 1998.

Campagna, Anthony S. *The Economic Consequences of the Vietnam War*. New York: Praeger, 1991.

Campbell, Angus. *The Sense of Well-Being in America: Recent Patterns and Trends*. New York: McGraw-Hill, 1981.

Carr, E. H. *The Twenty Years' Crisis, 1919–1939*. New York: Harper & Row, 1946.

Chandrasekaran, Rajiv. *Imperial Life in the Emerald City: Inside Iraq's Green Zone*. New York: Alfred A. Knopf, 2007.

Chomsky, Noam, and Edward Herman. *The Washington Connection and Third World Fascism*. Boston: South End Press, 1979.

Cobb, James C. *Away Down South: A History of Southern Identity*. New York: Oxford University Press, 2005.

Corson, William R. *The Consequences of Failure*. New York: W. W. Norton, 1974.

Dallas, Gregor. *1945: The War That Never Ended*. New Haven: Yale University Press, 2005.

Diets, Bob. *Life After Loss: A Practical Guide to Renewing Your Life After Experiencing Major Loss*. 4th ed. Cambridge, MA: DaCapo Press, 2004.

Dueck, Colin. *Reluctant Crusaders: Power, Culture, and Change in American Grand Strategy*. Princeton, NJ: Princeton University Press, 2006.

Eckstein, Otto. *The Great Recession*. New York: North Holland Publishing Co., 1978.

Fitzgerald, Frances. *Way Out There in the Blue: Reagan, Star Wars and the End of the Cold War*. New York: Touchstone Books, 2001.

Frum, David, and Richard Perle. *An End to Evil: How to Win the War on Terror*. New York: Random House, 2003.

Fukuyama, Francis. *The End of History and the Last Man*. New York: Free Press, 1992.

Gaddis, John Lewis. *Strategies of Containment: A Critical Appraisal of Postwar American Security Policy*. New York: Oxford University Press, 1982.

———. *Surprise, Security, and the American Experience*. Cambridge, MA: Harvard University Press, 2004.

Galbraith, Peter W. *The End of Iraq: How American Incompetence Created a War Without End*. New York: Simon & Schuster, 2006.

Gray, Colin S. *Another Bloody Century: Future War*. London: Weidenfeld & Nicolson, 2005.

Halberstam, David. *The Powers That Be*. New York: Alfred A. Knopf, 1979.

# Further Reading

Halper, Stefan, and Jonathan Clarke. *America Alone: The Neoconservatives and the Global Order.* New York: Cambridge University Press, 2004.

Hanson, Victor Davis. *Carnage and Culture: Landmark Battles in the Rise of Western Power.* New York: Doubleday, 2001.

Heilbrunn, Jacob. *They Knew They Were Right: The Rise of the Neocons.* New York: Doubleday, 2008.

Herring, George C. *America's Longest War: The United States and Vietnam, 1950–1975.* 2nd ed. New York: Alfred A. Knopf, 1979.

Hibbbert, Christopher. *Redcoats and Rebels: The American Revolution Through British Eyes.* New York: W. W. Norton, 1990.

Holsti, Ole R., and James N. Rosenau. *American Leadership in World Affairs: Vietnam and the Breakdown of Consensus.* Boston: Allen & Unwin, 1984.

Hopf, Ted. *Peripheral Visions: Deterrence Theory and American Foreign Policy in the Third World, 1965–1990.* Ann Arbor: University of Michigan Press, 1994.

Horne, Alistair. *A Savage War of Peace: Algeria 1954–1962.* New York: New York Review Books, 2006.

Iklé, Fred Charles. *Every War Must End.* 2nd ed. New York: Columbia University Press, 2005.

James, Lawrence. *The Rise and Fall of the British Empire.* New York: St. Martin's/Griffin, 1994.

Johnson, Chalmers. *Blowback: The Costs and Consequences of American Empire.* New York: Henry Holt & Co., 2000.

Johnson, Dominic D. P., and Dominic Tierney. *Failing to Win: Perceptions of Victory and Defeat in International Politics.* Cambridge, MA: Harvard University Press, 2006.

Johnson, Robert H. *Improbable Dangers: U.S. Conceptions of Threat in the Cold War and After.* New York: St. Martin's Press, 1994.

Kagan, Robert. *Dangerous Nation.* New York: Random House, 2006.

Keegan, John. *A History of Warfare.* New York: Alfred A. Knopf, 1993.

Kissinger, Henry. *Diplomacy.* New York: Random House, 1994.

———. *Ending the Vietnam War: A History of America's Involvement in and Extrication from the Vietnam War.* New York: Simon & Schuster, 2003.

————. *The White House Years*. Boston: Little, Brown, 1979.

Kübler-Ross, Elisabeth. *On Death and Dying*. New York: Touchstone Books, 1977.

Lamb, Christopher Jon. *Belief Systems and Decision Making in the Mayaguez Crisis*. Gainesville: University of Florida Press, 1989.

Lehman, John. *Making War: The 200-Year-Old Battle Between the President and the Congress Over How America Goes to War*. New York: Scribners, 1992.

Leiner, Frederick C. *The End of Barbary Terror: America's 1815 War Against the Pirates of North Africa*. New York: Oxford University Press, 2007.

Lomborg, Bjorn. *Cool It: The Skeptical Guide to Global Warming*. New York: Alfred A. Knopf, 2007.

London, Joshua E. *Victory in Tripoli: How America's War with the Barbary Pirates Established the U.S. Navy and Shaped a Nation*. New York: John Wiley & Sons, 2005.

Mandelbaum, Michael. *Ideas That Conquered the World: Peace, Democracy, and Free Markets in the Twenty-First Century*. New York: Public Affairs, 2002.

McInnes, Colin. *Spectator Sport War: The West and Contemporary Conflict*. Boulder, CO: Lynn Rienner, 2002.

McNamara, Robert S. *In Retrospect: The Tragedy and Lessons of Vietnam*. New York: Random House, 1995.

Mearsheimer, John J. *The Tragedy of Great Power Politics*. New York: W. W. Norton, 2001.

Mercer, Jonathan. *Reputation and International Politics*. Ithaca, NY: Cornell University Press, 1996.

Morganthau, Hans J. *Politics Among Nations: The Struggle for Power and Peace*. 5th ed. New York: Alfred A. Knopf, 1973.

————. *Vietnam and the United States*. Washington, DC: Public Affairs Press, 1965.

Mueller, John. *Overblown: How Politicians and the Terrorism Industry Inflate National Security Threats, and Why We Believe Them*. New York: Free Press, 2006.

————. *Quiet Cataclysm: Reflections on the Recent Transformation of World Politics*. New York: HarperCollins, 1995.

————. *Retreat from Doomsday: The Obsolescence of Major War*. New York: Basic Books, 1989.

————. *War Presidents and Public Opinion*. New York: John Wiley & Sons, 1973.

Murray, Williamson, and Alan R. Millett. *A War to Be Won: Fighting the Second World War*. Cambridge, MA: Harvard University Press, 2000.

Nixon, Richard M. *No More Vietnams*. New York: Arbor House, 1985.

Nordlinger, Eric A. *Isolationism Reconfigured: American Foreign Policy for a New Century*. Princeton, NJ: Princeton University Press, 1995.

Nye, Joseph S. *Soft Power: The Means to Success in World Politics*. New York: Public Affairs, 2004.

Packer, George. *The Assassins' Gate: America in Iraq*. New York: Farrar, Straus & Giroux, 2005.

Parker, Geoffrey. *The Army of Flanders and the Spanish Road, 1567–1659*. 2nd ed. New York: Cambridge University Press, 2004.

————. *Spain and the Netherlands, 1559–1659: Ten Studies*. Short Hills, NJ: Enslow Publishers, 1979.

Podhoretz, Norman. *Why We Were in Vietnam*. New York: Simon & Schuster, 1982.

————. *World War IV: The Long Struggle Against Islamofascism*. New York: Doubleday, 2007.

Press, Daryl G. *Calculating Credibility: How Leaders Assess Military Threats*. Ithaca, NY: Cornell University Press, 2005.

Quester, George H. *American Foreign Policy: The Lost Consensus*. New York: Praeger, 1982.

Rosecrance, Richard. *The Rise of the Trading State: Commerce and Conquest in the Modern World*. New York: Basic Books, 1986.

Sagan, Scott D., and Kenneth N. Waltz. *The Spread of Nuclear Weapons: A Debate*. New York: W. W. Norton, 1985.

Schivelbusch, Wolfgang. *The Culture of Defeat: On National Trauma, Mourning, and Recovery*. New York: Metropolitan Books, 2003.

Schlesinger, Arthur M., Jr. *The Imperial Presidency.* Boston: Houghton Mifflin, 1973.

Schwartz, Barry. *The Paradox of Choice: Why More Is Less.* New York: HarperCollins, 2004.

Shawcross, William. *Sideshow: Nixon, Kissinger and the Destruction of Cambodia.* New York: Simon & Schuster, 1979.

Siegel, Marc. *False Alarm: The Truth About the Epidemic of Fear.* New York: John Wiley & Sons, 2005.

Stiglitz, Joseph E., and Linda J. Blimes. *The Three Trillion Dollar War: The True Cost of the Iraq Conflict.* New York: W. W. Norton, 2008.

Suskind, Ron. *The Price of Loyalty: George W. Bush, the White House, and the Education of Paul O'Neill.* New York: Simon & Schuster, 2004.

Taft, Robert A. *A Foreign Policy for Americans.* Garden City, NY: Doubleday & Co., 1951.

Telhami, Shibley. *Power and Leadership in International Bargaining: The Path to the Camp David Accords.* New York: Columbia University Press, 1990.

Tuchman, Barbara W. *A Distant Mirror: The Calamitous 14th Century.* New York: Alfred A. Knopf, 1978.

———. *The March of Folly from Troy to Vietnam.* New York: Ballantine Books, 1984.

Tucker, Robert W., and David C. Hendrickson. *Empire of Liberty: The Statecraft of Thomas Jefferson.* New York: Oxford University Press, 1990.

———. *The Imperial Temptation: The New World Order and America's Purpose.* New York: Council on Foreign Relations Press, 1992.

van Heerden, Ivor, and Mike Bryan. *The Storm: What Went Wrong and Why During Hurricane Katrina.* New York: Viking Penguin, 2006.

Wann, Daniel L., Merrill J. Melnick, Gordon W. Russell, and Dale G. Pease. *Sports Fans: The Psychology and Social Impact of Spectators.* New York: Routledge, 2001.

Watts, William, and Lloyd A. Free. *State of the Nation 1974.* Washington, DC: Potomac Associates, 1974.

Weintraub, Stanley. *Iron Tears: America's Battle for Freedom, Britain's Quagmire: 1775–1783.* New York: Free Press, 2005.

Wheelan, Joseph. *Jefferson's War: America's First War on Terror, 1801–1805.* New York: Carroll & Graf, 2003.

White, Ralph K. *Nobody Wanted War.* New York: Doubleday, 1968.

Woodward, Bob. *Bush at War.* New York: Simon & Schuster, 2002.

Woodward, C. Van. *The Burden of Southern History.* Baton Rouge: Louisiana State University Press. 1968.


ARTICLES/CHAPTERS

Andreopoulos, George J., and Harold E. Selesky. 1994. "Assessing Recovery." In *The Aftermath of Defeat: Societies, Armed Forces, and the Challenge of Recovery*, edited by George J. Andreopoulos and Harold E. Selesky, pp. 1–9. New Haven: Yale University Press.

Biddle, Stephen. "Seeing Baghdad, Thinking Saigon." *Foreign Affairs*, vol. 85, no. 2 (March–April 2006), pp. 2–14.

Campbell, C. J. "Running Out of Gas: The Time of the Wolf *Is* Coming." *The National Interest*, no. 51 (Spring 1998), pp. 47–55.

Copeland, Dale C. "Do Reputations Matter?" *Security Studies*, vol. 7, no. 1 (Autumn 1997), pp. 33–71.

Desbarats, Jacqueline, and Karl D. Jackson. "Vietnam 1975–1982: The Cruel Peace." *Washington Quarterly*, vol. 8, no. 4 (Fall 1985), pp. 169–82.

Fettweis, Christopher J. "Credibility and the War on Terror." *Political Science Quarterly*, vol. 122, no. 4 (Winter 2007–08), pp. 585–615.

Foster, Gaines M. "Coming to Terms with Defeat: Post-Vietnam America and the Post–Civil War South." *Virginia Quarterly Review*, vol. 66, no. 1 (Winter 1990), pp. 17–35.

Geyer, Michael. "Insurrectionary Warfare: The German Debate About a Levée en Masse in October 1918." *Journal of Modern History*, vol. 73, no. 3 (September 2001), pp. 459–527.

Gholz, Eugene, Daryl G. Press, and Harvey M. Sapolsky. "Come Home America: The Strategy of Restraint in the Face of Temptation." *International Security*, vol. 21, no. 4 (Spring 1997), pp. 5–48.

Gholz, Eugene, and Daryl G. Press. "Energy Alarmism: The Myths That Make Americans Worry About Oil." *Policy Analysis*, no. 589 (April 5, 2007).

Herring, George C. "The 'Vietnam Syndrome' and American Foreign Policy." *Virginia Quarterly Review*, vol. 57, no. 4 (Autumn 1981), pp. 594–612.

Hixson, Walter L. "Containment on the Periphery: George F. Kennan and Vietnam." *Diplomatic History*, vol. 12, no. 2 (April 1988), pp. 149–64.

Holsti, Ole R. "The Study of International Politics Makes Strange Bedfellows: Theories of Radical Right and Radical Left." *American Political Science Review*, vol. 68, no. 1 (March 1974), pp. 217–42.

Hopf, Ted. "Soviet Inferences from their Victories in the Periphery: Visions of Resistance or Cumulating Gains?" In *Dominoes and Bandwagons: Strategic Beliefs and Great Power Competition in the Eurasian Rimland*, edited by Robert Jervis and Jack Snyder, pp. 145–79. New York: Oxford University Press, 1991.

Jervis, Robert. "Domino Beliefs and Strategic Behavior." In *Dominoes and Bandwagons: Strategic Beliefs and Great Power Competition in the Eurasian Rimland*, edited by Robert Jervis and Jack Snyder, pp. 20–50. New York: Oxford University Press, 1991.

———. "Political Implications of Loss Aversion." In *Avoiding Losses/Taking Risks: Prospect Theory and International Conflict*, edited by Barbara Farnham, pp. 23–40. Ann Arbor: University of Michigan Press, 1994.

———. "Theories of War in an Era of Leading Power Peace." *American Political Science Review*, vol. 96, no. 1 (March 2002), pp. 1–14.

Jespersen, T. Christopher. "Kissinger, Ford, and Congress: The Very Bitter End in Vietnam." *Pacific Historical Review*, vol. 71, no. 3 (August 2002), pp. 439–73.

Kahneman, Daniel, and Amos Tversky. "Prospect Theory: An Analysis of Decision Under Risk." *Econometrica*, vol. 47, no. 2 (March 1979), pp. 263–91.

Kristol, William, and Robert Kagan. "Toward a Neo-Reaganite Foreign Policy." *Foreign Affairs*, vol. 75, no. 4 (July–August 1996), pp. 18–32.

LaFeber, Walter. "The Last War, the Next War, and the New Revisionists." *Democracy*, vol. 1, no. 1 (January 1981), pp. 93–103.

Laird, Melvin. "Iraq: Learning the Lessons of Vietnam." *Foreign Affairs*, vol. 84, no. 6 (November–December 2005), pp. 22–43.

LeoGrande, William M. "A Splendid Little War: Drawing the Line in El Salvador." *International Security*, vol. 6, no. 1 (Summer 1981), pp. 27–52.

Logevall, Fredrik. "First Among Critics: Walter Lippmann and the Vietnam War." *Journal of American–East Asian Relations*, vol. 4, no. 4 (1995), pp. 351–75.

Luttwak, Edward N. "Iraq: The Logic of Disengagement." *Foreign Affairs*, vol. 84, no. 1 (January–February 2005), pp. 26–36.

Maliniak, Daniel, Amy Oakes, Susan Peterson, and Michael J. Tierney. "Inside the Ivory Tower." *Foreign Policy*, no. 159 (March–April 2007), pp. 62–68.

McMahon, Robert J. "Credibility and World Power: Exploring the Psychological Dimension in Postwar American Diplomacy." *Diplomatic History*, vol. 15, no. 4 (Fall 1991), pp. 455–71.

Mueller, John. "The Essential Irrelevance of Nuclear Weapons: Stability in the Postwar World." *International Security*, vol. 13, no. 2 (Fall 1988), pp. 55–79.

———. "The Iraq Syndrome." *Foreign Affairs*, vol. 84, no. 6 (November–December 2005), pp. 44–54.

Parker, Geoffrey. "Why Did the Dutch Revolt Last Eighty Years?" *Transactions of the Royal Historical Society*, 5th ser., vol. 266 (1976), pp. 53–72.

Podhoretz, Norman. "The Case for Bombing Iran." *Commentary*, vol. 123 (June 2007), pp. 17–23.

Pollack, Kenneth M., and Ray Takeyh. "Taking on Tehran." *Foreign Affairs*, vol. 84, no. 2 (March–April 1995), pp. 1–7.

Porter, Gareth, and James Roberts. "Creating a Bloodbath by Statistical Manipulation." *Pacific Affairs*, vol. 61, no. 2 (Summer 1988), pp. 303–10.

Puchala, Donald J. "Of Pirates and Terrorists: What Experience and History Teach." *Contemporary Security Policy*, vol. 26, no. 1 (April 2005), pp. 1–24.

Rauch, Jonathan. 2003. "Will Frankenfood Save the Planet?" *Atlantic Monthly* (October 2003), pp. 103–8.

Reuveny, Rafael, and Aseem Prakash. "The Afghanistan War and the Breakdown of the Soviet Union." *Review of International Studies*, vol. 25, no. 4 (October 1999), pp. 693–708.

Schlesinger, Jr., Arthur M. "Back to the Womb? Isolationism's Renewed Threat." *Foreign Affairs*, vol. 74, no. 4 (July–August 1995), pp. 2–8.

Seabury, Paul, and Alvin Drischler. "How to Decommit Without Withdrawal Symptoms." *Foreign Policy*, no. 1 (Winter 1970–71), pp. 46–64.

Shannon, Vaughn P., and Michael Dennis. "Militant Islam and the Futile Fight for Reputation." *Security Studies*, vol. 16, no. 2 (April 2007), pp. 287–317.

Simon, Steven. "America and Iraq: The Case for Disengagement." *Survival*, vol. 49, no. 1 (March 2007), pp. 61–84.

Slater, Jerome. "The Domino Theory and International Politics: The Case of Vietnam." *Security Studies*, vol. 3, no. 2 (Winter 1993–94), pp. 186–224.

Tang, Shiping. "Reputation, Cult of Reputation, and International Conflict." *Security Studies*, vol. 14, no. 1 (October 2005), pp. 34–62.

Telhami, Shibley. "The Return of the State." *National Interest*, no. 84 (Summer 2006), pp. 110–14.

Waltz, Kenneth N. "The Politics of Peace." *International Studies Quarterly*, vol. 11, no. 3 (September 1967), pp. 199–211.

Zeidenstein, Harvey G. "The Reassertion of Congressional Power: New Curbs on the President." *Political Science Quarterly*, vol. 93, no. 9 (Fall 1978), pp. 393–410.

# INDEX

# Index

# Index

# ABOUT THE AUTHOR

In 2008, Christopher J. Fettweis returned to Tulane University's Department of Political Science in New Orleans following three years of teaching U.S. foreign policy and grand strategy at the Naval War College in Newport, Rhode Island. He is the author of *Angell Triumphant: The International Politics of Great Power Peace*, which will be published in 2009, and a number of articles on U.S. national security strategy that have appeared in a variety of journals and newspapers. He has made many appearances in the national media discussing the way forward in Iraq, among other things.

He and his wife, Celeste Lay, live in New Orleans with their baby girl, Lucy, and a particularly annoying dog.